You've Got to Be
Carefully Taught

You've Got to Be Carefully Taught

Learning and
Relearning
Literature

Jerome Klinkowitz
With a Foreword by Kurt Vonnegut

Southern Illinois University Press
Carbondale and Edwardsville

Library of Congress Cataloging-in-Publication Data

Klinkowitz, Jerome.
    You've got to be carefully taught : learning and relearning literature /
Jerome Klinkowitz ; with a foreword by Kurt Vonnegut.
        p. cm.
    Includes bibliographical references (p.).
        1. Klinkowitz, Jerome. 2. English teachers—United States—Biography.
    3. English literature—Study and teaching. 4. Literature—Study and
    teaching. I. Title.

PE64.K56 A3 2001
820'.71'1—dc21
ISBN 0-8093-2403-2 (alk. paper)   00-054764

Red—how do you like the sound of a thousand dollars a week? Can't find a substitute? To do what? Teach English? What "teach English"? People speak English already!

—Mark Harris, *Bang the Drum Slowly*

Contents

Foreword

Jerome Klinkowitz is thirty years my junior but a longtime friend by now. He has published three books for each of mine, including novels and histories and memoirs, and his academic works have occasionally praised something I myself have done. So be it.

I, too, have been a member of several English faculties: in the Writers Workshop at the University of Iowa, in the company of such world-class writers as Nelson Algren and Richard Yates and Jose Donoso and Vance Bourjaily, and then solo at Harvard, and then with the famous Joseph Heller at the City College of New York, and presently solo at Smith College. In every English department, I have heard deeply concerned shoptalk by Ph.D.'s in which I and my fellow writers could not participate. It wasn't about literature itself, but about faculty politics, about perks and prizes and promotions and sinecures, and even wealth and fame, which may be achieved by those engaged for lifetimes in higher education.

Dr. Klinkowitz has himself played the nonteaching games of academe so successfully that he is, one is tempted to say, rich beyond the dreams of avarice. But he is nonetheless moved at this point in his life to suggest that those games, beginning with the often grim enterprise of earning a doctorate, have in fact caused many teachers to convey to students that reading great writing is a solemn chore rather than, as its authors had hoped, delightful and surprising. Put another way: is it possible that so many students find literature tedious because their teachers obviously, despite theatrics to the contrary, find it so?

Klinkowitz's antidote for such ennui, as much an occupational hazard for teachers of literature as the bends are for deep-sea divers, has been to befriend and celebrate writers who are still among us, to demonstrate to himself and colleagues and students that literature defines itself as such to readers, long before it is embalmed, if ever, by theses and syllabi.

Kurt Vonnegut

Acknowledgments

In the more than quarter century I've taught at the University of Northern Iowa, its English department has become a pleasant and stimulating place in which to work. In telling the story of my own formal education in literature and how I had to relearn the process and devise ways to teach it, UNI has been exceptionally supportive of my work. At age fifty-five, I am old enough to have served under three university presidents, three provosts, three graduate deans, seven collegiate deans, and eight department heads, and every one of them has made my terms of duty easy while offering generous financial support for virtually anything I wanted to do, from literature itself to allied interests in baseball, music, and the narratology of World War II's air combat. My three previous years at Northern Illinois University saw much help, too, specifically in the mentorship of James M. Mellard. There have been times at both schools when things were not very pretty, but out of it came a better way to teach.

A series of grants from the UNI Graduate College has made this book possible, with Associate Dean David Walker finding the money and Mary Ann Hesse keeping the bookwork straight. My department head, Jeff Copeland, is the unsung hero of this book. Had he been born half a generation earlier and been my boss in 1972, the happy ending to my story would have come along more quickly. Thanks, Jeff.

You've Got to Be Carefully Taught

Introduction

"You've Got to Be Carefully Taught" is a pretty-sounding but cruelly meaningful song from the Rogers and Hammerstein musical *South Pacific*. It was popular as a show tune when I was a little kid and as a protest song of sorts a decade and a half later. But whether as an impressionable youngster or twenties-ish proper radical, I never really grasped its message. You would think I'd have learned the lesson by age fifty-five, when I decided to write this book, but I was two-thirds through before the title occurred to me. By then, I had finished with the nasty stuff about my wasteful miseducation and shameful distraction by the snake pit of academic politics and had begun transcribing the joy of what I teach these days, the only course I've taught since finding my own solution to the English department's curricular wars twenty years ago, Introduction to Literature. Here, in the happiness I'd found, came the pretty music for these ironies of wisdom.

Age fifty-five is when English professors are supposed to have it good, and I surely do. *You've Got to Be Carefully Taught* is my fortieth published book; I hold a "distinguished scholar" chair that pays the proverbial six-figure salary for research plus teaching two half-semesters, a couple courses that I choose. Plenty of other tenured radicals with doctorates from the sixties share this good fortune. Some have withdrawn into the quiet of tiny advanced seminars with the cream of their graduate school's crop. Others have renewed their commitment as activists and are quite literally teaching in the streets. But to the best of my knowledge, I'm the only one who has avoided both the cozy seminar rooms and the confrontational hassles outside in order to teach two sections each time 'round of the supposedly bonehead, general education, nonmajor, requirement-fulfilling course that most freshman hate so much they put it off 'til they're seniors, Intro to Lit. Professors of any rank rarely teach this course; attitude problems on both sides have made it the fodder for temps and adjuncts, or at the very best an endurance contest for probationers working their way to tenure. That I not only ask for it but refuse to teach almost anything else is a scandal to

some, a grandly romantic gesture to others. The book I offer here explains how it is really something else: the prototype for the complete reinvention of what English departments, if they wanted to, could be doing.

The premise comes from my own experience with what a miserable job literature faculties are doing today and also from my understanding of how so many projected reforms, coming as they do from brilliant theorists at the most prestigious universities, have the chance of a snowball in hell when applied to simply average schools like the one at which I teach. There is no trouble finding wide agreement with either of these points, although I wish more thinkers would put the two together. As for my conclusion, that the principles of an inductive, open-ended course devoted to the process of literature replace the present product-based organization of the curriculum, its sense takes a little time to register. The idea itself is revolutionary and has more than a touch of anarchy to it. But if people who work with literature—and that includes anyone who digests a book with something other than speed-reading consumption in mind—think back on how the techniques for doing so were taught to them and how their own manner of enjoyment had to be figured out independently of that, my suggestions will seem far less radical. That's why this book gives equal time to each of the three phases: how literature has been traditionally taught (chapter 1), why piecemeal changes and larger attempts at reform have failed (chapter 2), and what a successful re-presentation of the subject actually looks like in practice (chapter 3). All three are couched in my own experience—again so that there can be a bedrock of practicality to the project. My own education and initial teaching experiences were so unremarkably average that no one would think to write about them, but because of that, no one has given himself or herself the solid platform from which to speak. What's different—radically, but only apparently anarchistically different— is the third part, my response. But what makes it so accessible and usable is how it grows out of an experience so many average people share.

In chapter 1, the story of my education proceeds with attention to key details about literature and how I read it (as told to and otherwise). Books and magazines, especially readable magazines like *Collier's* and the *Saturday Evening Post,* were always plentiful at home, but what I was most adept at was "reading" TV. Early television shows had strong senses of narrative and seriality to them, and all this I followed with intense interest. I knew there was a difference to my style of reception, because my parents noted

things I did—things involving temporal sequence and motif—while my brother enjoyed the medium more as something for consuming an hour—as spatial an affair as filling up a glass with Kool-Aid and draining it again and again in an orgy of unquenchability (and of no apparent satisfaction). But before you think this meant I was born as a protopostmodern, realize the Milwaukee suburb we lived in was still so rural that for me first grade started in a one-room schoolhouse, Valley View School in the Town of Greenfield. Eight rows, eight grades, taught by one teacher who handled each subject four times over, taking two rows at a time for history, arithmetic, or whatever in advancing sophistication for grades one and two, three and four, five and six, and finally the big kids in seven and eight. As she moved on, we shrimps in the first two rows were left with homework. Some of us did it; others followed along with the increasingly mystifying story transpiring to our right. As remarkable and as occasionally profitable as this system was, it only lasted a year, with separate classrooms built in the school's basement next year and individual grades split by the time I left after fourth, so quickly had Greenfield grown.

For me, grade school was the first eight years of the fifties, and in the fall of 1954 I transferred with my closest friends to the newly opened Catholic school in Hales Corners. Here was another outdated but still fiercesomely operative cliché of old-fashioned education, this time the parochial variety: unqualified teachers. For fifth grade, it was a joy, giving us Brother Francis, his bare feet shod in thin leather sandals and wearing nothing else but a coarse brown robe, belted with a rope. For him, literature was music, its texts being some archaic forms predating even Gregorian chant, and except for Religion, this music filled our entire class day. Sixth grade gave us a graduate student (in classical Greek, of all things) whom we terrorized; in seventh, we got it all back from a literal Sister Mary Battle-Axe. Only for eighth grade, when the parish realized we were almost totally unschooled, did we get Sister Alphonsine, who'd been a high school principal in Chicago, to mold us into shape. But by then, I'd been taught every wrong-headed way there is to read literature—or, better yet, not been taught much of anything at all.

So most of my experience with writing happened on my own. I loved historical narratives, only now (I realize) for their sense of story—at the time I was shunning anything else as made up and therefore worthless. World War II aviation memoirs thrilled me, particularly European theater stuff, so as a ten year old, I subscribed to the *Royal Air Force Flying Review,*

devouring each monthly issue (given mostly those days to first-generation accounts of the war from RAF and Luftwaffe sides) and ordering volumes from its book club, texts like Johnnie Johnson's *Wing Leader* and Adolf Galland's *The First and the Last*. Baseball was my other love, taking part in the self-consciously grand narrative of the Milwaukee Braves. What crescendoing highs, what plummeting lows—and not just on the field, for the city's people made it a genuinely cultural event. These influences, from early fifties TV and the one-room school house to Catholic school and the education I had to make for myself from airwar stories and baseball, are the gist of chapter 1.

High school (at the all-city Marquette University High School downtown), college (at Marquette itself), and graduate school (finishing with a doctorate at Wisconsin, out in Madison) was a sixties story, a matter of slowly coming to awareness of other values. The big thing here was learning how it was not just ourselves but an entirely new culture taking shape out there. At Marquette High, I kept sneaking away to the university, twenty blocks down the main drag; from MU, which when I got there seemed stifling, I made early forays to Madison, where life seemed much finer. A journalism major lasted me less than one college semester, and history was handled best as a minor, the avocation that I preferred it to be. It was the lifestyle of English professors rather than their subject that attracted me, and by now I could see how literature mirrored what had been in fact the historiography (rather than plain history) I'd always loved. But no one at either MU or UW was ready to teach me this, which is the point I had not quite learned at the end of this first chapter, when I turned in my dissertation (on Hawthorne, for the venerable and visibly ancient Harry Hayden Clark) in September 1969 and sped off to my first faculty meeting at Northern Illinois University.

At Marquette, I'd been taught New Criticism (with honest-to-Godness doctrine making explicit what Brooks and Warren only implied). Wisconsin, where I stuck with professors like Harry Clark (who was crowding seventy), gave me old-style literary history. I can't say these were the methods I used when teaching my American lit classes at Northern Illinois, because for me they weren't "methods" at all. If they were, I would have recognized all the contradictions between these two. Instead, as I sailed merrily into a decade of becoming the privileged English prof I'd always wanted to be, the specifics of New Criticism and old history dissolved— not that I'd ever really noticed them—in favor of just sitting down and

talking about what seemed to be happening in the novels, stories, poems, plays, and essays up for discussion. This meant matter both inside and outside the work, but neither of them religiously so. It was at Northern Illinois that I first saw some faculty members—associate professors, the most dangerous rank—making a cause out of one or the other. Who cares, I thought, but I did notice how a historically based "story of English" dominated the curriculum. Because American lit had less of a story, the department establishment downgraded it—at times they made me feel that in teaching Hawthorne and Melville, Howells and Twain, and certainly Fitzgerald and Hemingway, I was scarcely a step above coaching P.E. Hey, there was a story here! Hadn't these profs read F. O. Matthiessen? "That Communist?" they asked me in return—hadn't he killed himself in guilt over his lost ways?

As the ground floor in NIU's department was already filled with bright (if narrowly directed) careerists and the penthouse occupied by ignoramuses who liked boasting how they hadn't read a book since finishing their Ph.D.'s, I got out of there after three quick years. It was 1972 by now, with very little movement possible in the job market, well into its era-long collapse (I'd been hired a month before the disastrous MLA convention in Denver in 1968). But because I'd published, rather flashily so, and developed working relationships with a number of noteworthy writers, some other schools showed interest. Syracuse University administrators gave me a final-cut interview at their private club in the East Sixties, uptown from the cattle market of MLA; Wesleyan University officials actually flew me cross-country to Connecticut, where (I learned much later) Richard Ohmann tried but failed to convince his colleagues that my crudeness could be ground away (even he knew there was no chance of me having any polish, son of an Irish waitress and a Polish beer salesman that I was). What came through was an associate professorship at a place I'd never known existed, the University of Northern Iowa in Cedar Falls (where?).

How did this happen? Sitting with Jerzy Kosinski in his quarters at Davenport College, Yale, I was treated to stories not just about his childhood in Poland and young-man adventures in the underworld of New York but also about some prof named Dan Cahill, who was, with me, one of the few academics doing serious work on his fiction. He was a department head, Kosinski noted, adding that this was the kind of person I needed to know. The rest, as they say, is history.

Talk about writing one's way into a better job—though I had my quota

of scholarly articles in *Emerson Society Quarterly* (on Hawthorne), *Modern Fiction Studies* (Howells), and *Critique* (Faulkner), it was the trendy stuff on contemporary fiction that got me noticed. I shouldn't even say "contemporary," as that term was reserved for acknowledged writers such as Bellow, Malamud, O'Connor, Baldwin, Mailer, and the like. My people were, as I called them, "postcontemporaries," guys such as Kosinski, Clarence Major, Donald Barthelme, Ronald Sukenick, women such as Grace Paley and Susan Quist, writers on whom absolutely nothing had been written. Even Kurt Vonnegut, who'd just recently had best-seller success with *Slaughterhouse-Five,* was fifty years old, with an eight-book canon on which no work had been done whatsoever. They were postcontemporaries because serious critics had not noticed them and, even more so, because the bulk of their work was not yet written. By writing them, I was able to make contact, conduct interviews, borrow old manuscripts (such as William H. Gass's doctoral dissertation in philosophy from Cornell and Kosinski's two M.A. theses from the University of Łodz in Poland) and get leads on where forgotten bodies (such as essays and reviews) were buried. Essays and soon books of my own about them began flowing out of the Midwest like new Fords. Just recently turned from a teachers' college into a full-fledged seat of higher learning, the University of Northern Iowa was desperate for young profs who could publish. With my second book, *The Vonnegut Statement,* reviewed in *Time* magazine (its countercultural issue with Janis Joplin on the cover), I was set for life. UNI hired me as an associate professor when I was twenty-eight years old, then made me a full prof at age thirty-two, by which time I was the highest paid professor on campus (quite a trick in English when the school has a thriving business college, its accounting program ranked best in the country). Cedar Falls was a lovely place to live; the students were bright and sincere. Nothing could be finer, right?

Through the rest of the seventies, I continued teaching upper-level and graduate courses in the full range of American literature while doing most of my research on the postcontemporaries. Nearly all of them, from Vonnegut and Kosinski to Sukenick, Major, Raymond Federman, and Steve Katz, made visits for readings, symposia, parties, and transient cohabitation (with justification, I titled one of my early books about them *The Life of Fiction*). But as I proceeded this way, two things dawned upon me: that in both my classes and in my research, I was doing just what anyone who loves reading books and talking about them does, in pretty much the same

ways, but also that none of my colleagues, who seemed much more dedicated to department activities, was engaged in anything like this at all. This becomes the subject of chapter 2, how their worlds and mine became such radically separate entities.

This is just an introduction, not the whole argument, so let's cut to the chase. Because the doings of my own English department (and those of every other English department that I looked at, and vice versa—nominations for distinguished chairs here and there pleasantly surprised me a few times) began looking so disgusting, I opted out of the curriculum in favor of teaching just two sections of the course nobody else wanted, Introduction to Literature. Here was safe ground from everything I despised, including turf wars with colleagues, axe fights with administrators, and blinkered expectations from an increasingly dull (and shrinking!) body of English majors and grad students, nearly all of whom had responded to the petrification of our curriculum by studying to the exam. Why I had to get out (to save my sanity if not just my love for literature) is detailed in chapter 2; and though I make it sound like the department from hell, it was really the department from everywhere. Again, there's nothing truly radical in my view—just typical, but in ways too many of us are hesitant to express.

Okay, I was able to opt out because I was a rich guy, rich in both salary and privilege. But I did not turn my back on the subject, just on the way it was being taught. I could have amused myself and bored the few brighter students there were with a pair of introspective seminars on Hawthorne and Vonnegut, then gone home to drink beer. But I loved teaching lit, looking forward to my courses and having the time of my life in them. Despite its pressure to publish, UNI maintained a public image of being the school "where teaching comes first," and my teaching did; though our collective bargaining contract required student evaluations just once every five years, I had them done every semester I taught, and I got the college's highest scores (in a general education course that by tradition saw the instructors savaged). If I made some enemies on the faculty, this was how. Nobody begrudged me my salary or my light duties, and no one resented that I published; if I wanted to waste my time writing books, that was up to me. But those of us who published were supposed to be lousy teachers—after all, didn't we get those books out by stealing time from our students, and wasn't that why they themselves declined to write? My success in the classroom blew their theory all to hell and made them look bad

(and also drew attention to the fact that after teaching their 8:00 and 9:00 A.M. courses, some of my university colleagues were heading off to the real estate office, computer store, used-car lot, and in one case a lumber yard for a full day's work at a second career). This is getting pretty good, isn't it? Read about the whole sordid mess in chapter 2.

But there is life after the English department. Chapter 3 could well be an answer to the movie-lore paradox, "Is this Heaven? No, it's Iowa." Throughout the eighties and nineties, and with no end in sight, I've taught my sections of Intro to Lit with immense success and satisfaction. Why and how are detailed in loving length in this last full chapter, before winding up with some afterthoughts on the profession in general. A decade before *Field of Dreams,* I got involved with the local minor-league baseball team, as part of both my research and my teaching (the two soon became one, anyway). I also played in a blues band, for the same reasons. My working with living authors has continued apace, dragging me back into the department maelstrom to teach a single advanced course: Working with Living Authors. It was a great success, but I don't want to do it again. Keeping current with new writing has let me participate in the great curriculum wars my own way: since 1979, I've written the field's review for *American Literary Scholarship,* a project of the American Literature Section of the Modern Language Association that's published each year by Duke University Press, and in 1996, I was called on to do my period's reconstruction for *The Norton Anthology of American Literature.* Yet this latter type of work has a theoretical cast to it. As far as reinventing literature for the classroom, I've already done it on my own. Oh, what fun it is. *You've Got to Be Carefully Taught* shows how.

1
Education

Always a reader, I didn't start with literature. Instead, it was history, something important. Why invest time in things that were made up? For all the effort, wasn't it wiser to get on with what was real?

But because reading required some work, I went about it in ways that made history more like fiction. My aunt could speed read, typical of her talents as a career businesswoman, and during her visits, I'd wonder at how she could turn the pages of thick paperbacks as quickly as flipping through a picture magazine. Though easy, it didn't look like fun, with her face screwed in sharp concentration, lips set in a frown, brow knitted as if something were very, very wrong. She could just as well have been studying a balky balance sheet at an office in the chain of finance companies she supervised. The very quickness of it made it seem an onerous task, something to be got through as briskly as possible.

My own manner of reading spoke much more of leisure. The great amount of time it took was spent pleasurably, a short chapter in *Chief Black Hawk* or *Kit Carson and the Opening of the West* taking as long as an hour's math homework or mowing half of our yard. Because it was leisurely, my reading fixed on special pleasures. Not the least were the physical presence, texture, and even aroma of the book itself. To this day I will appreciate the feel of cloth bindings and heavier weight of paper, especially when deliciously porous. And the smell—even the acid bleaching of a cheap paperback has its appeal, together with the bonding glue. If a book has been expensively produced, the sensual joy is all the greater. That I read and collected books in series was another pleasure; lining them up was a sign of accomplishment and also of accumulating an apparent totality of knowledge. Not that I felt my understanding was encyclopedic—just that I'd mastered what the Landmark series, for example, had to say about the West;

another set of volumes might state the case differently, from bindings and print stock to orientation and mood. It was as much the historiography as the history that had me fascinated, and all of that took extra time to digest.

In grade school, "reading," as it was called, was one of my least favorite subjects, largely because it was so boring. Perhaps Catholic school was to blame, as everything seemed an excuse for religious instruction; in geography, we studied only Catholic countries, an endless array of anonymous places whose products were inevitably indigo, rice, and hemp. Reading exercises were worse, being little homilies of Catholic schoolchildren challenged by secularities of the world (with kindly nuns and a firm priest to the rescue). High school should have been different, and for most subjects, it was. Marquette University High School was deadly serious about Latin and Greek, for 2 percent of us would become Jesuits with a leg up on those languages for the Novitiate. Math was also strong, because of its intellectual nature. Only the sciences really suffered, thanks to a combination of churchly distrust and penury, our labs having little more than the leavings from old erector and home chemistry kits.

Freshman English was just as bad. I can't remember anything we read, just the image of Father Hauser: a hairless, reptilian-hued old priest with yellow teeth and bulging, rheumy eyeballs, who never left his desk and rarely lifted his elbows from their splayed position, which made him look like a pterodactyl at rest. Dactyls—that was what we studied, as most of our time was directed to metric scansion. Iambs, trochees, spondees: the whole nine yards. No words; just the beats. No wonder I can't remember a line of poetry from this year-long torture, much less any larger work of literature.

Obviously, it was literature we needed. My classmates were way ahead of me on this, one of them surprising me as much as the teacher by demanding a better curriculum. It was Mike Vater, probably the brightest in this top class in the best-ranked high school in the city, who popped the question.

"Father Hauser," he asked one day during the duller-than-dishwater second semester, when even the dactylic thumpings couldn't amuse the simpler of us, "when will our class be able to study not just the abstract principles of literature but read the works of its great modern masters, such as James Joyce and William Faulkner?"

The old Jesuit tried not to show the shock he was feeling, but his eyes did pop out a bit farther, like those of a newt roused from half-lidded contemplation on a spiky branch.

"Mr. Vater," he replied, even after five months of corrections mispronouncing Mike's name as the German for *father* rather than with the long *a* it deserved, "the writers you name are masters only of vulgarity and shame. With the principles this course of study imparts, you may go on in later life to appreciate the valid treasures of poetry, fiction, and the drama." He sounded the first syllable of this last word with a long *a,* the one missing from Mike's last name. "There should be no need," Father Hauser nodded with finality, "to waste these talents on the consumption of trash."

Mike didn't answer, but I could see the trouble he had containing his exasperation. As a "V" he was seated well toward the back, his view blocked by hulking Michael Mahoney and screened by the three O'Connors, unrelated and variously sized and shaped yet addressed by our teachers as "Primus," "Secundus," and "Tertius," respectively. But by his head shakings and sour looks, Mike Vater was doing all he could to convey how inadequate this answer was.

For my part, I shared Mike Vater's general sense but not his particulars. What was special about James Joyce? And why should Father Hauser be so upset about the author of "Trees," a poem read way back in sixth grade? As for "the masters of modern literature," that seemed awfully intimidating, something as heavy and abstract and daunting as the calculus awaiting us in Senior Math. But Mike's point was still well taken: this was Marquette University High School, and we were the cream of the crop, Greek and calculus and all. Surely, our English class should aspire to something higher than the "DA-duh-duh Dah-duh-duh" of a conga drum or badly tuned small engine.

What Mike Vater wanted came next year. Sophomore English for MUHS group 1 was taught by Mr. Thomas Collins, one of the young Jesuit scholastics teaching school for a few years between lower orders and ordination to the priesthood. Scholastics were in their midtwenties with an M.A. in their chosen fields. Most would stop there. But not Tom Collins. He'd already begun doctoral work; some said all he needed was his dissertation. Besides being named for a fashionable drink, he was quite the opposite of old Father Hauser: literally tall, dark, and handsome, and intellectually stylish to boot. Rather than using dull reading texts, he had us substitute *Time* magazine, studying articles from each weekly issue to learn the lucidly balanced way they were written. When we didn't understand the topicality, he explained it briefly. Throughout the year, he treated us not

as children but as adults, taking us into his confidence when Robert Kennedy addressed the student body on behalf of his brother's candidacy in that spring's Wisconsin Presidential Primary. There were reasons why he himself supported the senator from Massachusetts, Mr. Collins revealed. But he also explained why some of our more conservative parents might object to Bobby's appearance. It was what an older brother or trusted young uncle might say, and his manner made all the difference.

Taking note of *Time* style was a good idea. Even in 1960, it could be a subject for parody—soon Donald Barthelme would make his way into the *New Yorker,* with one such piece of mimicry, "Snap Snap"—but to the sophomore mind, it takes something brutally obvious to be noticed. This translated to the faculty's Democratic politics as well. Adlai Stevenson would have put us to sleep. Robert Kennedy, both in manner and on the issues Mr. Collins prepared us to follow, was exciting, and reading *Time* kept us in the game. With its emphasis on active verbs, the magazine taught us what a clear and simple sentence was; to choose the occasionally vibrant adjective was a perfect joy for any pimply sixteen year old. Marquette High, with its intellectually muscular tradition, was a school where brain power showed off as well as athletic prowess, and whipping off a *Time*-style paragraph counted as much as a ninety-mile-per-hour fastball or an arm that could throw touchdown pass sixty yards deep.

Second semester brought us a famous literary figure as well—not in person, but by means of personal anecdotes from someone we felt we knew. Mr. Collins had decided that the best exercise for our newly developed talents would be to encounter a contemporary master at length. Not "modern," I noted thankfully, for now I knew who James Joyce was and how difficult William Faulkner could be as well, for Mike Vater was jocking us all out the gym door by reading *Finnegans Wake* and *The Sound and the Fury* in tandem. Evelyn Waugh was the figure Tom Collins chose, a Catholic writer picked less for doctrine than to ease the principal's fear that the novel in question might be dirty. It was, and it wasn't. *The Loved One* was diabolically funny, wickedly comic in a way that sophomore minds love best.

As one of Waugh's more outrageous books, it was a perfect fit for a class like ours. But there was another reason for the choice: it was written in and about America, and scarcely a dozen years before. If Waugh were a haughty, superior Englishman, he matched up well with our Marquette sense of being elite; if he felt superior to California popwash, so did we.

His rancor was expressed in beautifully stylized language that seemed to burn off the page with its rare but sharply turned qualifiers (as our ponderings of *Time* style had taught us to see). This was living literature in and of our own culture and written in at least an approximation of our own language. Nothing needed to be footnoted, as our Latin and Greek cued us into the meaning of the heroine's name, Aimee Thanatogenus.

Best of all, this book was a relatively recent work, written within our still-young lifetimes by a palpably real author, a living presence in the lives of those around us. Waugh was a Jesuit favorite, converted by a member of the order and, as fashionably intellectual as well as sociocomic author, a prize addition to the Catholic canon. The soon-to-be-priest who taught us not only knew Waugh's works but had met the man personally. Just a year or two before, the author had visited Milwaukee and spoken at Marquette University, where Mr. Collins had been part of the social mix. And what a mix it must have been.

As we dipped into the first chapters of *The Loved One,* our teacher coached us on Waugh's habits and attitudes until we felt just as prepared as for meeting Robert Kennedy. How America in general grated against Waugh's brittle English propriety, how even our countrymen's best manners impressed the author as crudely uncivil, and how our freshly ecumenical brand of religion shocked the man's old style of Catholicism to the core— all this was a delight to hear about, especially as Waugh did anything but shun these things. Quite the contrary! His sense of the ridiculous drove him to seek out the worst in manners, morals, and quasi-religious wrinkles that characterized popular American life, as we'd be learning about in *The Loved One* soon enough. But first our teacher had a good story to share.

"One of Waugh's favorite places here in town is Avenue Church Goods," Mr. Collins told us, asking if we knew it. We surely did, as it sat in the 700 block of Wisconsin Avenue at the edge of downtown, beyond Marquette University and near the public library, museum, and auditorium-arena. "Every visit, he'd stop by for demonstration of the latest innovation for devotions."

Did this mean Evelyn Waugh was a piously devout Catholic, as we'd been taught to be in grade school but which the Jesuits at Marquette High were tempering with a wry superiority? Could this mean *The Loved One* would be a similarly inspirational book like some of the homely stories the good nuns had passed off as great literature? That made no sense at all, so Mr. Collins's teaser was working on our sometimes random attention.

"Mr. Waugh has his own style of adhering to the faith," our teacher counseled. "On his last visit to Avenue Church Goods, the clerk showed him an unbreakable crucifix."

Why an unbreakable crucifix, we wondered.

"I presume it was devised for travelers—and throughout his career, Mr. Waugh has traveled widely and written about it well, including some exotic trips to Africa. An unbreakable crucifix could be advantageous during the rigors of hard travel. Several of his fictive heroes spend time in the jungles of Africa and South America, for example, so as a social mannerist, he'd want to be up to date with such customs and equipment."

So he bought the device just a few miles down the street from Marquette University High School? Would it appear some day in one of his famous novels?

"Perhaps," Mr. Collins advised. "But for now, he uses it as lecture filler, an amusing story to warm up audiences, like 'a funny thing happened to me on the way to your campus this afternoon,' as on one day it really had."

What was funny about an unbreakable crucifix, we wanted to know.

"Oh, he made it sound hilarious," Mr. Collins insisted, adding that creating preposterous conditions was part of the writer's art. "You see, the clerk wasn't satisfied just telling how the object was unbreakable but insisted on giving a demonstration."

For this part of the story, Mr. Collins shifted to a slightly British inflection, pacing the account with clipped syllables and mugging a bit with a slightly outraged stare.

"'Let me show you the punishment this baby can take,' the chap boasted and taking the model from me, rapped it sharply against the metal counter. 'There, you see—not a scratch, not even to the figure!' Indeed, Our Savior's limbs and appendages remained smartly intact. No mere clerk could place a whack on Our Glorious Redeemer."

As we began laughing at the juxtaposition of language, Mr. Collins upped the accent and took on more of the Englishman's podium manner.

"Admitting this, however, was the wrong thing—just adding petrol to the man's fire, for now he threw the Lamb of God down on the floor and began kicking Him from corner to corner. I had to step back lest I have my ankle cracked. By this time, the fellow had reached a pinnacle of fury, and from the peak of his rage, he leapt down on the Sacred Tree and stomped it unmercifully. 'There!' he'd gasp in a strangled shriek of vindication, as with each crashing descent the windows shook, and frightened shoppers

glanced in with alarm. Finally, with his breath recovered and color turning back to normal from its purple hue, he picked up the business and returned it to my hands, smiling so sweetly in shopkeeperly obeisance and crooning the device's high praises. 'Unbreakable! Absolutely indestructible! A must for the well-equipped traveler!'"

With this about the author understood, our reading of *The Loved One* was a rich experience. I can surely date my beginnings as a literary critic to Mr. Collins's presentation of Evelyn Waugh. All the elements I'd later pursue as my chosen profession were here. The man's books were contemporary, almost all of them in print. Marquette High was smart enough to stock its school supply store with tempting paperbacks, such as histories and mythologies to supplement our Greek and Latin studies and the entire run of Waugh's double-volume paperbacks published by Dell. Before the semester was out, I'd purchased all of them for summer reading, from *Black Mischief* and *A Handful of Dust* to *Officers and Gentlemen* and *Put Out More Flags*. This was a habit I'd follow henceforth for every new author I liked, covering everything the person had written. For Waugh, this meant his biography of Edmund Campion and his various travel books. As a living contemporary, the man could not be exhausted by such research, so my quest was a living, vibrant thing. Hampel's Bookshop, a few doors down from Avenue Church Goods, stocked his *The End of the Battle* as a current title (a hardcover that cost me two weeks' lawn-mowing money the next year), and *Time* magazine reported how the author was at work on a three-volume autobiography, the first volume of which (*A Little Learning*) was well underway. Most important, he was personally accessible: Mr. Collins had met him and could fill in details; plus, we ourselves could walk the same streets and perhaps see the same hardy crucifix put through the wringer. All of this would be the method I'd use when studying and teaching my own discoveries twenty years later.

Other interests (and consequent methodologies) date from these days. Back in fifth grade, I'd begun subscribing to a British periodical, *Royal Air Force Flying Review,* and purchasing volumes of classic World War II air combat memoirs from their book club: masterpieces such as Johnnie Johnson's *Wing Leader* and Heinz Knoke's *I Flew for the Fuhrer,* which I read comparatively. During freshman year at MUHS, I discovered jazz, attending a Gerry Mulligan concert and next morning asking the bandmaster if I could play baritone sax; he started me out on clarinet, but soon I had a tenor saxophone and was playing in a combination rock and polka band,

working everything from sock hops to wedding dances. At the same time, I picked up *down beat* and the occasional *Metronome* and devoured the ongoing story of jazz. And what a living history it was: within one amazing month, Downer College, Shorewood High, and my own school hosted relatively intimate performances by Louis Armstrong, Duke Ellington, and the Miles Davis Sextet, featuring John Coltrane and Cannonball Adderley—the entire history of jazz, like being able to attend live readings by the authors of *Beowulf, The Canterbury Tales, Macbeth, Pride and Prejudice,* and *The Loved One,* all in the same short season. The tunes were great, the performances exceptional, and the solos out of this world. But it was the larger narrative sense of jazz that really thrilled me.

By my junior year at Marquette High, I felt literarily empowered, having mastered the narratives of three diverse areas: jazz, Battle of Britain air combat historiography, and Evelyn Waugh's career as a fictive satirist. For group 1's Junior English, we had an unusual assignment for a teacher, neither a scholastic (like Mr. Collins) nor an old warhorse of a nonacademic priest (Father. Hauser), but rather a bona fide professional in the field. F. Christian Keeler, S.J., was ordained and also had a Ph.D. Why he wasn't teaching at Marquette University itself or at Creighton, Fordham, Rockhurst, or Boston College escaped us. Only at the school year's end, when he suddenly disappeared from sight, did it occur to us that he might have been serving time among us lowly secondary students because of some glitch in his career.

As it was, his presence moved me that last step toward a true dedication to literature. Our first assignment was to write something about ourselves, probably so that Father Keeler would know with whom he was dealing. Having had a full dose of Evelyn Waugh, I wrote satirically and rather sarcastically about my family's Marquette tradition I was expected to uphold, reaching past my father, who had flunked out of Marquette University after a semester spent shooting pool in the student union, to my grandfather, Anthony Klinkowitz, "who, football in hand, had charged out of Marquette Academy in 1906." Father Keeler liked the tone, loved the imagery, and was delighted I'd found words to fit the ancient photograph I'd seen of "Tony Klink," as he'd been called, with the rest of the school's starting eleven. The paper came back covered with lines of encouragement summed up by an interesting imperative: "You have an obvious gift for writing. Develop it! And to do that, *read, read, read!*" I prided myself on how widely I read: not just literature (and then in canonically complete

batches) but all the World War II air combat memoirs, the jazz news and criticism, plus a fair amount of writing about baseball, the major league histories and fortunes of which I followed with particular care (complementing the squeaky clean Milwaukee Braves and their new County Stadium with forays to musty old Comiskey Park in Chicago). I disappointed Father Keeler by never equaling that exuberant first essay, but he continued thrilling me with his spirited interpretations of literature. It was from him that I learned how one could speak litcrit in a working-class voice. A large, red-faced, beefy man, he'd exaggerate his gruffness by transliterating lines of Shakespeare in the style of a Brooklyn cab driver, getting cheap laughs for his muggings but making points about the playwright's talent for communicating. There was nothing sissified about either producing literature or critiquing it, his method showed. This was tough stuff for tough people. Much later on, when I read Mark Twain and then Ernest Hemingway and eventually Frank O'Hara, I'd hear the same vernacular strength Father Keeler had brought to the business.

Meanwhile, the music continued. By the end of this junior year, I'd worked my way into one of the best local rock 'n' roll bands and was employed two nights a week as a musician. This made for its own narrative in the arts, and since we were all MUHS students (or ex-students, as our leader had graduated to Marquette U), the atmosphere remained intellectual. During what should have been the capstone to my high school English, Father Crowley's senior class for group 1, I diddled away the year distracted by jazz. He was an excellent teacher and handled literature all the right ways, but my attentions were elsewhere; my own reading and Father Keeler's teaching, I felt, had given me everything I felt I needed, so in typical MUHS tradition, I goofed off and only studied for the grade. Grades were desperately important: the more than two hundred members of my class were ranked by numbers, revised each semester, which like an English football league system placed us in groups declining from 1 to 7. On the basis of my entrance exam, I'd been put in group 3, but by Christmas was moved up to group 1, where (except for Senior Math) I stayed. Yet even within this vaunted first group, there was unstated competition for top spots. Much like baseball's amateur draft today, if you weren't in the top ten, you could kiss academic advancement goodbye, at least in terms of preferential treatment. By acing Father Crowley's class and avoiding the dreaded calculus, I made a strong finish and ended up number three in the whole school, a position way, way over my head. Jim Black, num-

ber one, copped a full-ride scholarship to Boston College, the Harvard of Jesuit universities. Tom Fox, number two, had a wicked fastball and won an athletic scholarship to Stanford, which after a year's brilliant classroom work he got converted to an academic ticket and studied on to become the editor-in-chief of the *National Catholic Reporter*. As for me, I had a rock band in Milwaukee with its MUHS members continuing on to Marquette U. I was having fun, learning music (and lowlife) from the inside, and earning more than MU's hefty tuition. My number-three ranking would get me excused from all the Mickey Mouse requirements, and my income as a musician meant I didn't need to comply with the good-boy requirements of a scholarship. So, tenor sax in hand, I honked, booted, and growled my way into the university my father had blown off so casually thirty years before.

While music was keeping me in Milwaukee, literature remained such an accustomed pursuit that I was shocked when my friends coming with me to Marquette U. declared other majors—Mike Vater in philosophy, Tom Repensek in French. We three had used our astronomical high school ratings to pass out of most freshman requirements, including composition, and were taking Albert Misseldine's honors class in lit, an introductory survey of sorts. After momentary seductions by journalism (so I could write) and ROTC (Lord knows why—maybe my RAF reading), I took the formal option for English, based on the happy news that with a Ph.D. one could teach it at university level without needing any education courses. In one fell swoop, as they say, I freed myself from journalistic methodologies (and ethics!), educationist foundations (and ethics!), and a likely death in Vietnam (I finally dropped out at the start of junior year when parade was shifted from 3:30 P.M. to 7:00 A.M. so that afternoons were free for gymnastic practice in "counterinsurgency warfare"—don't tell me the military didn't know Nam was coming!). Being a professor looked good, a lifestyle I was seeing from the inside thanks to my girlfriend's job as secretary of the philosophy department just upstairs from English.

I'm still surprised Albert Misseldine's class didn't keep Vater and Repensek in the fold, as in addition to his great material, the teacher himself was a treasure. "Albie," as we came to call him almost to his face, was a young Englishman from Birmingham with an M.A. earned at one of the red brick universities; he was over here as part of Britain's widely heralded brain drain. With his prematurely receding hairline, tortoise shell spectacles, and distracted, almost frazzled manner, he was just the type (right out of a Rich-

ard Lester movie) for a bunch of brainy honors students, and although the class was coeducational, it had much the feel of old group 1 back at Marquette High. Once again muscular intellectualism vied with good fun for filling up the class period and the discussions that spilled out into our real lives. We didn't shoot pool in the union—shooting bull about Albie and his literary favorites was better.

Albie's course compressed two semesters of freshman comp and another two of English lit survey into fifteen exciting weeks. Composition alone would have been ridiculous, for Tom Collins had taught us how to write three years ago. And having the lit dragged out over two semesters, as it would be for the quiz sections I'd handle just a few years later as a teaching assistant, was too tedious to imagine. As it was, Albie treated the history of English as something providing highlights to the more serious business of working with literature and writing about it. To show that he wasn't chauvinistic about his homeland's texts, and more likely reflecting the interest that brought him to our shores, he made *The Great Gatsby* our course's centerpiece. As usual, I established my own research by reading everything else by F. Scott Fitzgerald as well, from some schoolboy stories and *This Side of Paradise* to *The Crack Up* and *The Last Tycoon*. As Matthew J. Bruccoli must have been doing at the same time, I scoured old issues of the *Saturday Evening Post* for uncollected stuff. Dead for twenty-two years, Fitzgerald came alive for me in Arthur Mizener's critical biography and in a volume of letters I found remaindered in Chicago during a White Sox trip. As with Evelyn Waugh in high school, I had a shelf of resources to work with, including the knowledge that there was one work by this much-studied author that had not yet received attention: his play *The Vegetable,* existing in just a tiny first printing, one copy of which circulated from the MU library. Here, as a lowly freshman, was my first literary find.

That the play had been overlooked by critics was inexcusable. True, it was a failure, such an embarrassment that the author refused to let it be listed afterwards among his published works. But historically and biographically, it was crucial, written in 1923 at the height of its author's popularity; its popular failure sent him into exile abroad, where he summoned the remarkable artistic strength to craft *The Great Gatsby* in hopes of finding literary integrity. Uncovering something by a major figure that was critically untouched became a habit; five years later, in my first doctoral class at Wisconsin, I'd do a Faulkner seminar paper on *Knight's Gambit,* something easily placed in *Critique* as one of those worth-their-weight-

Reading, that is, if the experience was to be something other than a simple consumption, digestion, and regurgitation of the author's work. If the act of reading were a mere replication of the created text, my students and I were little more than photocopy machines, which wasn't the case at all, as the simplest pop quiz (which I never gave) or briefest discussion (which we did pursue at length) revealed massive distortions in even the most attentive response. *Thirty readings yielded thirty different books.* Everybody knew that even before the course began, and there was not much to do with it but toss out some Buddhist puzzles or come off sounding like comedian George Carlin, both of which happened unintentionally plenty of times during that first semester of teaching. But to pin down the differences was something else. Thirty readings came from thirty backgrounds, and even though those backgrounds could emerge in discussion, it was hard to work with such amorphous material. We could, however, establish some parameters for the first book up and then see how the second departed from them in favor of something else. No single work's integrity was challenged, nor need we digress into pointless debates about meaning (make that Meaning). What we could debate was that ever-open area of the space between.

That first fall semester at Northern Illinois University had me working harder than at any other point in my life, harder even than during the time I'd spent churning out my dissertation. Keeping up with nine hours and two preparations was enough to fill my days and evenings, too. Though stuck in an apartment, we still prioritized space. As pioneer farmers knew, the house doesn't pay for the barn, so for us the barn came first. Jonathan's crib could stay with us in the first bedroom, leaving the second as a study. With wall-to-wall, floor-to-ceiling bookcases (freshly made and walnut stained, best carpentry I've ever accomplished); well-positioned library table as a desk (drawers were distractions); a red telephone (my "hotline" to the professional world); soft, low lighting; and two comfortable chairs (one at the table, the other in a corner), it was the nicest room we had. The apartment's utilitarian nature here could be cloaked in a contemplative atmosphere. Thus, it didn't bother me to be holed up here most nights until midnight preparing for my eight and nine o'clock classes next morning. My Faulkner and Howells papers from Wisconsin were coming into print, and some afternoons were spent mining my dissertation for publishable pieces on Hawthorne. But most of my time went to "figuring out the teaching," something I'd been warned would consume the bulk of my first year.

Even if spring semester had brought me the expected course on my

in-gold publications for job interviews. Here in honors English I was not about to do anything original on Fitzgerald, even regarding a critically untouched work. Instead, I produced (as Albie Misseldine wisely suggested) a reputation study, surveying the contemporaneous reviews to discover why the times felt Scott Fitzgerald had gone so wrong. It was fascinating to see how commentators dealt with someone who only a decade after his death would be perceived as having great literary talent capable of yielding true masterpieces, but who had in *The Vegetable* produced a real stinker. Later on, I'd look to major artists' lesser works as a way of seeing their methods profiled so much more obviously in the rough and stayed away from teaching too many acknowledged masterpieces lest students be afraid to cast a critical eye.

As for my own writing, Albie was critical enough. For our first essay, I'd tried matching the panache displayed for Father Keeler two years before, showing off every fancy technique I knew. To my great chagrin, it came back graded C and blue-penciled throughout, so much as to say the C was overly generous.

Rather than listen to what my teacher had to say, I argued. Weren't these majestically done constructions a sign of both great art and intelligence? Didn't my ability to reel out subordinate clauses that had the look and feel of a diagrammed sentence speak for the nature of my thought, every turn of which was traced in exquisitely correct syntax?

"Did you have Latin in high school?" Albie asked, and I said yes, adding proudly that I was doing a fifth year here in college (not mentioning that my only motive was to win exemption from the two-year foreign language requirement—once again the Jesuits would wreck an entire curriculum to service the tiny percentage of students who might become priests).

"Well, it shows," he grumbled, and explained how a Ciceronic style was the worst thing possible for good plain spoken English.

"Plain spoken English?!!" In Ciceronic declamation, I parsed out all the reasons for writing with high style, insisting that giving way to plainness was to surrender one's intelligence.

"You like to use the library," Mr. Misseldine observed. "Go check out some of George Orwell's essays. Read his 'Politics and the English Language' for the theory, then follow up with 'Shooting an Elephant' and 'A Hanging' to see how he does it himself." My teacher paused to smile, lowering his gaze a bit to emphasize his thick-framed glasses and steep forehead above. "I don't think you'll find he surrenders his intelligence at all."

Encountering Orwell meant more than Mr. Collins's *Time* style and Evelyn Waugh put together, for here was clarity and art happening together. Mike Vater and Tom Repensek were already making jokes about what would happen and pranked me by withdrawing all the library's copies of *Burmese Days, The Road to Wiggan Pier,* and *Homage to Catalonia* before I could get to them. That was no problem, as I'd discovered Schroeder's Used Books on Wisconsin Avenue (across the street and up from Avenue Church Goods) and for thirty-five cents apiece could buy used paperbacks of nearly everything Orwell wrote. I bought *1984* new because it would be required for Dr. John Pick's modern British novel course, something few MU undergraduates (even nonmajors) missed. True, Orwell, like Fitzgerald, was dead, but his living influence was present in Albert Misseldine, who could have been any Orwell protagonist and was. Moreso than with Waugh, who'd impressed Tom Collins for various intellectual and aesthetic reasons, I could see in my first college teacher a person whose moral outlook had been shaped by a writer and whose growth and conduct were governed by such ideals. That is why all the blue penciling: Albie really cared about sound thoughts and clear expression, not for art's sake but for society's. Nobody ever lost his or her life for writing satire like Evelyn Waugh, at least not in an English-speaking country. Millions around the world did for having the courage to express themselves as honestly as George Orwell.

At MU, my English major was the traditional one, with only two courses in American lit: Joseph Schwartz's coverages of modern American poetry and fiction, respectively. The former might as well have been a British literature class, as great time was spent covering the Royalist-Anglican-Conservative aspects of T. S. Eliot's art and more than a smattering of Ezra Pound's fascism. Both were still alive, Eliot writing blurbs for Faber and Faber, Pound confined in St. Elizabeths mental hospital to save him from a trial for high treason. Dr. Schwartz was a dire conservative of the William F. Buckley variety and doted on the Eliot who stood against the vernacular and the Pound who (with Mussolini's help) opposed Roosevelt's New Deal. We read Robert Frost, Hart Crane, Wallace Stevens, and a little e. e. cummings ("i use capitals for EMPHASIS!") as well, but always from a strictly high-modern, antidemocratic view. The novel course was more popularly American, beginning with Sherwood Anderson and ending with Robert Penn Warren (whose excitement over Huey Long we had no way of understanding), with John Dos Passos along the way. For those considered the towering masters, Dr. Schwartz liked to vary choices each semes-

ter; by taking his class in the spring, I was stuck with *A Farewell to Arms* instead of *The Sun Also Rises, Tender Is the Night* over *The Great Gatsby,* and *Light in August* in place of *The Sound and the Fury.* Thus, except for Gatsby, which I read in Misseldine's course from a writerly point of view, I missed out on what I later learned to be the artistic strengths of the truly modern American novel in favor of books that in this teacher's hands became political examples. Yet Faulkner was still alive and Hemingway just recently dead, and through the Book of the Month Club I was able to buy and read *The Reivers* and *A Moveable Feast* as they appeared. A branch of the Milwaukee Public Library at my bus transfer on the way home provided me with brilliantly dustjacketed first editions of *The Hamlet, The Town,* and *The Mansion,* helping me appreciate how the man who'd grown old writing them could begin his novel with the words "Grandfather said:". Hemingway's memoir stumped me, as I knew few of the references. But nearly two decades later, it proved a guide to living the life of fiction in Paris, an experience that turned my work around as thoroughly as it had Hemingway's.

The other highlight, as anticipated, was John Pick's course The Twentieth-Century British Novel. Not "modern," because unlike its American cousin, Dr. Pick's course went all the way to the present, ending with Alan Sillitoe and John Braine, England's "Angry Young Men" contemporaries. Of course, everything about Dr. Pick suggested currency and immediacy. Like Albert Misseldine, he spoke with a British accent: pure Oxbridge, well behind Albie's attempt to regularize his own broader midlands speech. No matter that John Pick was a native of West Bend, Wisconsin, just forty miles north of our city and well within its orbit of sing-song Milwaukee-talk. He'd been educated at Oxford, and just as we were losing our "down by Schuster's where the streetcar turns the corner 'round" folk language at cosmopolitan MU, he'd left his in England, coming back with all the manners of actor George Saunders, whom he more than slightly resembled. He'd published a critical biography of Gerard Manley Hopkins with Oxford University Press and done an edition with Doubleday Anchor Books, bringing the late Victorian priest and poet to modern prominence. He'd married the countess of Malta as well, whose fortune let him teach for pleasure as a dollar-a-year man. There were stories of his and Cissy's honeymoon, a year spent back in England where Dr. Pick had written his scholarly magnum opus, only to see it go to the bottom with the *Andrea Dorria.* "Always make carbons of everything," he cautioned us, as he'd learned too late, "and ship them separately." But the line we treasured was from the

countess, time-capsuled by CBS radio dockside as she was lifted from the lifeboat: "Yes, John's all right, but my jewels, my jewels!"

Dr. Pick taught his course with an impeccable sense of style: not just the British accent and physical pose, but deft little sartorial touches like changing his watchband each day to match his bow tie. All of this was carried on with great fanfare before a lecture hall of two hundred students. His course, The Twentieth-Century British Novel, was the department's great moneymaker, eclipsing Introduction to the Theater from Father John Walsh and even Dad Murphy's Ethics, which packed them in for theater and philosophy, respectively. The man had great stage presence, playing up his looks and manners so effectively we sometimes thought we were watching a black and white classic on late night TV. Like many English majors, I considered myself superior to such monkeyshines and vowed I'd never teach that way myself, either with the showboating manner or at the breakneck pace of one book every week. It took the more perceptive Mike Vater to make the point: Dr. Pick was making this literature enjoyable and hence accessible to a wide range of MU undergraduates. "That's how we produce an educated student body here," he assured me. "How else are engineers going to learn about such things? Would you want them totally ignorant of the writing of their times?" Thirty-five years later, I'd be defended the same way.

What I found most impressive about Dr. Pick's course was its thrilling immediacy. Here was a man who had not just studied literature or worked on these writers from a distance but had worked *with* them. For older figures at the course's start, he could not have had personal involvement, but he made it seem as if he had. For D. H. Lawrence, whose *Sons and Lovers* was reputed to be hot stuff but turned out not to be, Dr. Pick used a remarkable device to lend intimacy. It happened on the Wednesday of Lawrence week, when our lecturer (in red-striped tie and watchband) drew to a close early, climaxed by his request that all of the young women in the class please leave. We tittered, then laughed—this was, after all, the professor who in last year's MU yearbook had let himself be photographed tossing handfuls of term papers down the department stairwell, successive steps of which were marked A, B, C, D, and F, and who in next year's *Ahoya* would be pictured in a Beatles sweatshirt. But within a moment, we knew he was serious, for he insisted with an unaccustomed scowl that the ladies leave forthwith. This accomplished, he called us fellows down from our customary backrow perches to gather around his lecture stand, which was

in fact the demonstration table in this science auditorium needed to hold his course's oversubscription.

"When Lawrence and his wife, Frieda, sojourned in New Mexico," Dr. Pick announced, "the author painted a series of erotic, some say pornographic renderings in watercolor." He paused to survey us, making sure no women had lingered. "I have a folio of them here and invite you to peruse . . ." Engineers and English majors alike crowded around to see, in obvious disappointment, that the erotic subjects were the same sex as ourselves and that the pornography consisted in the exaggerated size and detail given to their genitals. Wait 'til Mike Vater hears about this, I thought. But the intention was well taken: our teacher had something intimate associated with D. H. Lawrence, and with subsequent authors the material became more pertinent (and shareable with the coeds). There were stories about a figure's campus appearances here and at nearby schools, some of them randy bouts with alcohol and women; more immediately, there were personal letters, candid snapshots, and inscribed first editions. Our own professor was a player in this world-class game, reminding me that literature was far from being a dead subject.

By carrying heavy loads and taking classes two summers, I was able to graduate a semester early. My motive was purely economic: I was paying Marquette's exorbitant private school tuition myself, working sometimes as often as six nights a week with increasingly professional rock and rhythm and blues bands and was getting married in the January of what would otherwise have been my senior year. A teaching assistantship paid two hundred dollars per month and, more important, remitted tuition—plus it would move me closer to full-time employment as a bona fide professor of lit.

Being a grad student didn't mean that much difference in the style of course work, other than having less of it, but a teaching assistantship gave me legitimate standing in the world around which I'd been lurking ever since my fiancée (now wife) had taken a job as philosophy department secretary upstairs from English. Much of the humanities faculty had offices in a massive block of Victorian apartments called the "Granmorra." Towering ceilings, tall fireplaces, and large bay windows abounded. The men and women whose profession to which I aspired might well have been characters in a Henry James novel, for every time I saw them, it was in some type of social repose: taking mail, chatting with the staff, sharing morning or afternoon coffee, and breaking open bottles of Scotch at department parties my boyfriend status made it possible for me to attend.

My own teaching was miraculous, happening only because (for the

moment) Marquette had no doctoral program in place, thanks to some accreditation hassle. With other M.A. candidates, I was able to teach quiz sections broken down on Fridays from the mass lecture course surveying English, and I was glad to share them, including coffee-time talks and classic grad student parties. Many of my colleagues were extending these years to accommodate other hopelessly unremunerative interests, such as painting, acting, and playing folk music. It made for a vibrant community, a small and yet diverse enough group that there was something special for each of us to do. The fact that I was earning money as a professional at my own avocational pursuit made me more commercial, but my abilities to talk lit and jazz kept me within the pale.

As a graduate student, I took two more American lit courses. One was a seminar on Emerson and Thoreau, which seemed more like philosophy and was; here one of the advanced students, Mac Davis, took over the Mike Vater role of being three steps ahead of everyone, wowing the teacher and going on to a University of Chicago Ph.D. and academic fame. Hawthorne, Melville, and Twain I picked up with lesser lights in another course from Dr. Schwartz, and it too became more philosophical and historical than strictly literary. While most of my Marquette profs were ostensibly Brooks-and-Warren-style New Critics, when it came to any American course, they felt compelled to justify its worth by turning it into a history of politics and thought. As Mike Vater had dismissed the field as only slightly better than a major in physical education, I could appreciate the strategy. But Mike had finished his first and last college English course by having Albie Misseldine let him write his term paper in French, even as he was taking his first-ever class in it, so that he could sharpen his skills; he was studying German, too, and doing a philosophical methods course paper in that language. With a Yale doctorate in philosophy just around the corner, he was not the right person for me to be listening to any more, but I did and avoided the other Stateside courses. Most of my work was in English lit, including remarkable Chaucer and Shakespeare seminars from an ancient visiting professor just retired from one of the Boston universities, Harvard-educated Harold Ogden White, the first college teacher to make something of my talents. Most likely, he was pleased by my Marquette High manners, which conveyed immense respect for authority and age, but thinking that I'd impressed him intellectually gave me a boost for planning doctoral study. Here I was, cutting the mustard with someone from the Cambridge elite.

Because several of my regular MU profs had degrees from Wisconsin,

and thanks to the Madison campus's proximity just ninety miles West, the UW doctoral program was a popular destination for our M.A. grads. Compared to Marquette's cozy little department, with its quaint habits like the chairman wearing Harris tweeds and walking matched Borzoi hounds across campus, Wisconsin looked to be very big time. Its faculty consisted of last names—Quintana, Hughes, White, Rideout, Clark—that were stamped on the spines of our own well-used textbooks. And Madison itself outclassed dingy, folksy Milwaukee, beating it out by miles in sophistication and beauty. My advisers said I should apply to three schools, so I also wrote to the State University of New York–Buffalo and the University of Illinois. Illinois paid more, nearly twice as much to TAs as did Wisconsin, while Buffalo offered Leslie Fiedler.

Why did I want to work with Fiedler? In studying for my comprehensive exams by filling in gaps in my coverage, I'd read more American lit and fell in love with it. The Reader's Subscription Book Club had sent me *Love and Death in the American Novel* for joining, and according to habit, I followed up my happy reading of it by checking out everything else Fiedler had done to date, including *An End to Innocence, No! In Thunder,* and *Waiting for the End.* There was also the lure of an accelerated program and a better level of teaching (lit not comp). Buffalo had become my first choice, so imagine my chagrin when just before the customary April 1 announcement date, I received a letter from SUNY's admissions office asking why on earth I wanted to study in their doctoral program when I was fifty-one years old and had racked up just one college semester of Fs and Ds back in the fall of 1930? My God—the Marquette registrar had sent out my father's transcript instead of mine!

Before I could panic over a possibly similar mistake with Wisconsin, their letter came, awarding me the teaching assistantship I'd requested, a first-round choice. In relief, I was prompted to accept at once. My profs urged waiting for Illinois, as some applicants were being given full-ride fellowships with no teaching duties, but when a week passed, I believed I'd been passed over in their first cull, so I sent my formal acceptance to Madison. On my way home from the post office, I stopped at the jazz store and bought a record to celebrate: not my customary Gerry Mulligan album but a Jazz Crusaders LP with more funk and wiggle to it, expressing my exhilarated mood. Playing it today always makes me feel that way again.

Three weeks later, the mailman woke us up in our apartment near campus with the special delivery letter from Urbana. Illinois had somehow botched its first round notifications and was getting offers out only now.

I was a top choice with better money and more perks than from Wisconsin. I didn't feel bad writing back that I'd already committed to Madison, for if Illinois had screwed up this, they could falter on other things as well. Years later, I'd see doctoral candidates from other schools be messed up just this way, while Wisconsin went to amazing lengths facilitating each stage of my work. Ever since then, I've always tried to work with people who are similarly on the ball. Conversely, the minute I sense there's idiocy at hand, the affair is history.

So it's safe to say I was fated to attend UW, thanks to a pair of mistakes that could have ruined me had SUNY or Illinois been my exclusive goal. Everything happens for the best: at Buffalo the rising faculty star was Raymond Federman, whose innovative fiction and freewheeling criticism would have puzzled and repulsed me in 1967 (but when discovered late in 1970 became part of my first postdoctoral activity and the foundation of my career). Illinois would not have been the place to have a romance with the American romantics; Brit lit ruled the roost down there, so different from Wisconsin, where forty years before American literature had first been taken seriously (and where a half century of the field's leaders would be educated). Plus, Chambana was no Madison, I was warned; no ridgetops of mystic Indian mounds with glimpses of five sky blue lakes through the oaks and pines. Not for the first or last times would apparent misfortune turn out to be my very best luck.

But first, there was the matter of M.A. exams. It was a single day's affair in midsummer, comprising a morning's objective exam on the length and breadth of literature in English followed by an afternoon writing essays on three set pieces, announced as *Macbeth,* "Tintern Abbey," and (as an eye-opening surprise) Philip Roth's still-new *Goodbye, Columbus (Portnoy's Complaint* was yet to be published, so the young author was not yet on the *Index of Forbidden Books).* New Critical training I'd received was perfectly applicable to Roth's well-made novel, and in working out schemes of approach, I was pleased at how rationally the book could be broken down into its structuring elements and then deftly put back together again. As far as its philosophy and literary history, they were my own, so there was nothing else but the work's aesthetic to study.

The exams were taken a month after we'd moved. At Marquette, my wife and I had rented an old apartment just half a block from campus, one door down Fifteenth Street from Wells, where third-shift bars, a Chinese restaurant, a tiny grocery, and a busy shoe repair shop served a borderline community being squeezed out by the university (today what was our sec-

ond-floor apartment's space is occupied by the video game lounge of the new student union). Our move in June of 1967 was another potential misfortune that turned out well. That summer the building would be demolished for urban renewal; had we needed to stay another year in the area's tight rental market, we would have been screwed. As it was, the city of Milwaukee was paying moving expenses for displaced tenants, and their allowances covered anywhere in Wisconsin. Hence, the professional movers we could never have afforded hauled our stuff to Madison, including the stove and refrigerator we purchased for a token five dollars apiece. This meant we could rent an unfurnished house, which we did on a beautiful tree-lined hillside of residential streets a lovely three-mile bike ride from campus. Briar Hill Road, which was as nice as it sounds, bordered the upper-class neighborhood of Nakoma, where period theme mansions of the twenties and thirties housed some of my future professors. At the end of our street was the university arboretum, stretching for miles around the shore of Lake Wingra. To this day, it remains the nicest address I've ever had, all for $130 a month. Though it almost doubled what we'd paid on Fifteenth Street, the peace and beauty were worth it. It was here I brushed up on the canon and reread (several times each) the Shakespeare play, Wordsworth poem, and Roth novella—all at a leisurely pace, as we had saved enough money to take the summer off. Though nervous enough to run a slight fever, I drove back to Milwaukee for the late July exam and aced it, getting a pass-with-high-honors citation.

In September, my classes and Elaine's job began. In booming Madison, her skills gave her the pick of executive secretary jobs, but she wisely turned down a high-paying one at a deadly serious agency in favor of becoming secretary to the associate chairman of the UW speech department, which also included theater. Here she replicated her happy social life from Marquette and continued for a year and a half before quitting to have our first child. By then, I'd raced through all my course work and won a second-year no-duties fellowship, which meant making just one monthly visit to campus to pick up my check. Over this final spring semester, I'd study for the doctoral comprehensive exams and during the summer write my dissertation. That it was a world's time record for finishing did not concern me, as the requirements were easily fulfilled or compromised. Once again, I dodged learning a foreign language by getting credit for my college Latin, letting my adviser believe I would use it for a study of Robert Lowell's Catholic poetry, an easy argument to win as I scheduled our conference five minutes before his customary lunch at the University Club. I crammed

a reading knowledge of French for my second language and passed the ETS exam because its passages were on current politics, something I knew inside out from reading the *New Republic* every week.

Prerequisites were also something I blithely ignored. For my first semester, I took one advanced course (John Conder's Realism and Naturalism) and two seminars: Faulkner from Walter Rideout and what I thought was Harry Hayden Clark's Hawthorne. The problem was that for Mr. Clark's course I had read the previous year's description, a misunderstanding that helped me keep an earnestly straight face as I argued my way in. Imagine the scene when on the first day of class I was met by the stares of nine doctoral candidates, most of them in their early thirties and program residents for years, as I took my seat in what was Mr. Clark's exploratory dissertation seminar.

It was a special colloquium set up to let finishing students test their ideas for a doctoral thesis by floating them as a free-ranging abstract. For the first meeting, Mr. Clark, well into his sixties, slightly stroke-enfeebled and only casually conscious of his status as one of the field's founders back in the twenties, asked us one by one to summarize our topics. Because I was seventh or eighth to speak, I had time to improvise an outline, based on what I'd hoped to do had the class in fact been on Hawthorne: how in most of his novels the author defines ideal humanity by what it is not and how the admittedly problematic ending to *The House of the Seven Gables* is flawed by Hawthorne here resisting this trend.

I don't think many of the other students heard me. Five- and six-year veterans of the program, all they could think of was who the hell I was. Mr. Clark's sustaining pose in recent years had been one of winsome befuddlement, which in this case let the inappropriateness of my presence go right over his head. Instead, he began stammering about how important it was to avoid negativity in characterizing Hawthorne's thought, a point he was still making a year and a half later when I actually wrote the dissertation for him, my proposed title *(Hawthorne's Negative Definition of Humanity)* long abandoned in favor of something more winningly positive.

Mr. Clark's seminar went like the Faulkner class and subsequent courses, with others getting more involved with the educational busywork, while I shot directly for publication. This manner came easily because Elaine and I had removed ourselves from campus life. At Marquette, we'd feasted at the center of it, socializing like graduate students as early as freshman year thanks to her inside-the-department job; once married, we lived practically above the store. In Madison, though, we stayed on the outside, liv-

ing well beyond the TA realm in a suburban world and family lifestyle that looked forward to what we were rushing to become. I looked like a radical, of course, and was typically far left in my politics but couldn't fathom why some grad students hated UW as much as the war and considered it as culpable as that other acronym, LBJ. Going back to the university after hours was like an expedition, such as when Don Lichty (the self-professed Madison lifer) took us to see the Paul Butterfield Blues Band at a small club called "The Factory." When we did interact with guys such as Don, it was as a missionary project, trying to save him from his sometimes dangerous activism (he was a disillusioned army vet and meant it) and Mike Krasny from his junk food diet and "serial monogamy." What social world we had beyond this consisted of dinners with two other married couples from the program, the husbands of which shared a corner TA office with Lichty and me. But cases like Krasny were more fun. I'd met him at registration, where he was near collapse from a devastating pulmonary infection; I took him to student health and invited him out to Briar Hill Road for fresh orange juice, the first he'd had in a decade. As for the graduate student ghetto down on Mifflin Street, a region known as "Miffland," we only saw it when driving Mike or Don home.

My doctoral course work at Wisconsin, hurried as it had been, was exclusively American, and its strict historical approach gave me a solid basis in the canon and a command of the larger frame. When organizing my own classes later on, I'd be entranced by what Robert Spiller's book had called "the cycle of American literature," reflected in the book title. It was reassuring how everything had a categorical fit and a role to play in the almost Hegelian progression from the colonial to the revolutionary and from there through romanticism, realism, naturalism, and modernism. That the modern was ending before our eyes was not yet evident. Although Wisconsin's English department had a journal, *Contemporary Literature,* it was dedicated to the brainy obscurantism of its editor, L. S. Dembo, a specialist on Pound's Cantos. (John Enck, the magazine's more present-oriented founder, had died the year before.) Writers favored were Thomas Pynchon and John Barth, especially the Barth of *Lost in the Funhouse,* who visited us with his pair of stereo tape decks. This was not at all my cup of tea—or rather mug of beer, as Barth was the tea drinker and given to such phrases. On my own, I'd read John Updike as an undergraduate and Kurt Vonnegut as relief from the pressure of M.A. seminars. During the summer of 1968, I audited John Lyons's lecture course Contemporary American Fiction and learned all about manners and morals. Updike, Bellow,

and Malamud all seemed more palatable than Barth and Pynchon, but for Lyons's favorites, there didn't seem much to probe for. So I remained a steadfast nineteenth-century advocate, feasting on Hawthorne and tasting Howells for the flavors of transition and contrast.

All went smoothly in our cozy little bungalow, as Socialist Worker Lichty had called it. My last fall semester of classes had me preparing for fatherhood, another masterpiece of lucky timing. Earlier that spring, I'd faced a problem with my country's politics: the Vietnam buildup was about to cost a generation of students their draft deferments. Up to this point, guys like myself had prolonged our exempt status through grad school until reaching age twenty-seven, at which point age took us out of the pool. Now, a new law was taking effect. If one asked for a student deferment, it meant waiving all future excuses, including fatherhood and age. I remember sending in my own annual reapplication the winter before figuring that I was setting myself up for an eventual draft, but what else could I do? Opening the Selective Service board's reply, I lost a heartbeat when I read the first line. My request for a renewal of my student deferment was being denied! The second sentence revived me: I was being given an occupational deferment instead. All of this was on the board's own initiative.

It wasn't hard to figure out. Giving me what I asked for would have made me certain for the draft. Having an occupational deferment kept my options open, at least for the moment. If I became a father, I was still eligible to be free of the army for good. The reason for my local board's action was clear. The public high school I would have normally attended was a poor one and not accredited; few of its graduates had gone on to college, giving the board a huge supply of military fodder. I'd gone to Marquette High instead and thus was rare enough to be protected so far and worth saving for the future. This was social engineering, or "channeling," as the Selective Service policy manual called it. Fatherhood would exempt me, if Elaine and I could manage it before the spring semester expired. Her pregnancy report was mailed to the draft board with less than a week to spare.

Another combination of good luck and smart timing let me leave Wisconsin not just a parent but with a job in hand, something quite rare for the doctoral class of 1969, which was the first to experience the sixties sellers' market collapse. Back in October of 1968, no one knew it was coming or was willing to admit it if they did; it took the disastrous MLA convention in Denver that Christmas to reveal what a vast surplus of candidates there was for the pitifully few positions available. I remember Stan Hen-

ning's job market session with us in September, saying how we should limit our applications to only the best schools (Columbia, Berkeley, and the like) and from the piles of offers we'd surely receive to consider only those paying ten thousand dollars or more with a maximum load of nine hours and two preparations. Avoid small private colleges, he warned—they'd demand too much work and offer insufficient resources, and so forth.

Therefore, when Northern Illinois University showed up with its English department "Steering Committee" to interview anyone and everyone, all my friends sneered. The few of us who did go through a session said we were doing so simply for the interview practice.

My own turn went well, especially when I told the committee members I had an article on Faulkner accepted for publication, with others on Howells and Hawthorne circulating. Theirs was a big department already, and to meet wildly ambitious enrollment projections and staff a wildfire doctoral program, they were intending to double that, hiring a dozen new assistant professors annually for the next three years. The meeting ended with everyone beaming. The assistant chairman, Arnold Fox, walked over to me and gave me a warm embrace, saying I would definitely be hearing from them soon. Later on, I'd learn Arnold thought I was Jewish and therefore suitable for an ethnic slot they were dedicated to filling (Fox himself was the only Jewish professor on campus). Everyone else seemed to be eating up the publications. As it turned out, they made offers to every UW student interviewed. I alone accepted. The figures were right: ten thousand dollars, nine hours, two preparations. All but one would be advanced courses. Only after the debacle at Denver did anyone in Madison think I'd done the right thing.

Doctoral comprehensives were scheduled for the second week of April. It had been a beautiful early spring, and for weeks before, Elaine and I had been out with our tiny son, Jonathan, backpacking him for bike rides or pushing him in his stroller through the stately residential streets of Nakoma and around the duck pond at the arboretum. I was the luckiest guy on earth, with a happy family, nice home, ideal occupation (being paid a teaching assistant's salary just to study for comps), publications already accepted, dissertation soundly conceived, and first job appointment in hand. Indeed, I was the only UW Ph.D. in English coming out that year who'd snared a job thus far, so deep and widespread had the market crash been. Years later, some of these same people would still be working in other fields, waiting to get a start in their chosen profession. They also happened to be the ones who, like the undergraduate radical clique in their composition classes,

couldn't distinguish between Dow Chemical and the University of Wisconsin Regents, or between the department's professors and the Pentagon's war planners. One could be a committed socialist without trashing the campus, I believed, and I had been so happy just to be in Madison that I could never understand this hatred of the university. So in getting a job (with my radical looks and attitudes notwithstanding), I felt some vindication along with the obvious good luck.

In getting ready for the exams, I'd set up a strict program of study and was disappointed only in the impenetrability of the modernist critiques I'd planned to read. Modern was one of my three areas, after eighteenth and nineteenth centuries—all American, of course, as had been all of my classes. The written exams lasted a week, filling Monday, Wednesday, and Friday mornings, and were considered quite daunting. People failed regularly and had to be approved for a retake next semester. But with no classes to take or teach, I was in the best possible position to prepare, and prepare I did.

What happened was that I overprepared, most fatally right through the Sunday night before. Today, I advise students facing such tests to wind up their studies several days if not weeks before and after that to concentrate on relaxing themselves into top psychological, emotional, and physical shape. I did just the opposite and paid for it. In better all-around condition months before, thanks to my ideal schedule, I blew it all by needless last-minute acceleration that by the last weekend had me a nervous wreck and by Monday morning a physical and mental basket case. Somehow, I dragged myself down to Bascom Hall, passing the National Guardsmen occupying campus since the police riots a few weeks before. Once into the eighteenth-century exam, I settled down. It was mostly poetry and critically reductive; what can be problematic about Philip Freneau? Biking home along my favorite route had me almost relaxing, but once in the house, I froze up. Through the kitchen and past our living room was the hallway and door to my study—an incredible perk for someone my age, but there it was, a reminder of the pressure cooker I'd created for myself. I shuddered to look at it, filled as it was with preparation materials and emblematic of the crisis at hand.

Though we could scarcely afford it, I suggested eating out, getting some Kentucky Fried for a duck pond picnic. Then we strolled Nakoma 'til Jonathan's nap time, snarfed leftover chicken for dinner, and sat out in the back yard in the early dusk. Refortified, I spent Monday night and all day Tuesday cramming.

Wednesday's test went much the same. One question surprised me,

asking for a survey of critical interpretations of the American West. I knew the examiners wanted something on Henry Nash Smith, but his *Virgin Land* was one of those texts I'd let go until too late. Much of Tuesday had been spent staring at its red cover and black title stamping. That was all I knew about it: its colors. But this was better than nothing, so I faked my way through an answer, improvising what Nash should have said (even if he didn't). Mark Twain, for example, was a vernacular writer; the curator of his papers surely knew that. I felt comfortable enough with the results that I made it home that afternoon in fairly reasonable shape.

That night and Thursday, however, were miserable. Long-term big-picture worry set in, ranging from all I hadn't said on the first two exams to what kind of career I could have if a Ph.D. were denied me. I thought back over all my work through the years, beginning with English classes in high school and developing through the happy departmental life I'd shared at Marquette plus the doctoral courses and already-secured job and was crushed that it would all come to nothing based on just one set of exams. The Northern Illinois position dropped down to term instructor at eight thousand dollars per year if I didn't arrive with degree in hand, and there was no way of getting on the tenure track without it. All along, even before snaring the appointment, I'd felt firmly that I had to finish up while in Madison, a habit of making clear-cut decisions I seemed to have been born with. On reflection, I was sure I had failed the first two exams, given how shabby my performance ranked against all the information I knew existed. Being immersed in more than I could command, I now realized, was a bad way to prepare; better that my time had been taken up with teaching and course work. But it was too late now. Most of all, I was totally drained and could not imagine facing one more day of such torture.

Thankfully, Thursday was gorgeous weather, midseventies and clear, bringing out blossoms everywhere, so we spent the whole day outside. Even after dark, I was loath to come in (there were books inside!); therefore, I walked by myself the two blocks over to Nakoma. For an hour I roamed the neighborhood, staring through windows into brightly lit interiors thrown open to the warm spring night. Even garages had their charm, with yard tools hung on walls and mowers ready for weekend duty. It was an appealing domestic lifestyle portrayed here, one that several top UW English profs shared, and now it seemed forever out of reach to me.

Soon I was walking down Seneca Place, where in midblock stood Harry Hayden Clark's gambrel-roofed colonial cottage. Like all the other homes,

it was open and illuminated; on the side porch that served as his study, I could see Mr. Clark at his desk, back to me, busy with some papers. I stood there several minutes, taking it all in, then began to cry. That lasted a few minutes, too, until I worried he might turn around, so I hurried away. By the time I reached home, I felt a little better, the emotional release draining off some tension. At least it would all end tomorrow. Had I been facing the old program's routine of five days' exams instead of three, I'm sure I would have collapsed entirely.

Friday morning I awoke like a condemned man on gallows day. I arrived at school early and spent some time visiting with Elaine's friends in the speech department office. Their happy workaday manner unnerved me: how could they be so casual with such doom impending, when the world as I knew it was just about to end? At 9:00 A.M. I reported to the English graduate office and picked up my exam. As on Monday and Wednesday, I walked down the hall to a small conference room and got seated with my ballpoint pens and bluebooks. Totally unsupervised, I could have cheated at will; but this was Wisconsin, where in Navy and Harvard tradition the professors were called "Mister" and honor was a way of life, so any cribbing was unimaginable. As it was, the eerie solitude made the prison atmosphere more apparent. No one cheats on death row.

Not that any amount of cheating could have helped. Opening the test envelope, I was struck cold. There, neatly mimeographed on porous blue paper, was the question: just one for this whole area of twentieth-century American literature on which I was to write four hours. My preparation wasn't lax, as at Marquette I'd taken Dr. Schwartz's survey courses in both poetry and the novel, while here in Madison I'd studied Faulkner with Walter Rideout's elite seminar and audited John Lyons on postwar fiction. But it was, all told, my weakest area.

Had there been some variety, some choice, I could have faked it. The son of a Milwaukee beer salesman can fake anything. But there was not. Instead of the panoply of historical minutia and flatly reductive criticism that had characterized the eighteenth- and nineteenth-century exams, here was a doozy of a puzzler: "Citing and employing the most important of recent such texts, including but not limited to Claude Levi-Strauss's *The Savage Mind,* J. D. Watson's *The Double Helix,* Norman O. Brown's *Life Against Death,* and the most important poststructuralist works in linguistics, write a well-developed essay explaining how the literature of our era reflects trends in social and scientific thought."

Oh shit. J. D. Watson's *The Double Helix,* Levi-Strauss, Norman O. Brown—who's zooming who? The only thing I knew about this stuff was what I'd seen by sludgy British intellectuals in the *New York Review of Books,* essays I'd learned early on in my subscription to skip.

Unlike the question with Henry Nash Smith's *Virgin Land,* I didn't know the jargon for this new style of litspeak and thus had no chance in hell of faking it. That scared me, but what made me angry was that the profs who wrote this question obviously were making fake moves, fakier than the Harlem Globetrotters in their opening patter—and not for fun. Thirty years later, I can imagine the answer and appreciate how what really did happen in "the literature of era" would have made it total drivel. I knew the young assistant and associate professors responsible and had shunned them for all of my two years here. Friends would rhapsodize over the gobbledygook being spooned out in such courses and during the chatter afterwards. I'd turn back to the elegance of eighteenth- and nineteenth-century literature as idealized by Harry Hayden Clark, a figure more than twice these junior faculty members' age and light-years ahead of them in experience, the experience of working with literature rather than just bull-shitting about it. I was teed off, and I was shaken, for because of this non-sense my future in the profession was about to dissolve.

I wasn't sure what to do, but one thing was certain: I could not sit in this suddenly claustrophobic room. Leaving the test materials on the table, I left, wandering back to the speech department, where the morning's easy society had blended into the day's first coffee break. I had some. Wasn't I supposed to be writing my last doctoral exam? Well, yes—but I wasn't quite ready for it. From the secretaries' worried glances, I could tell they knew how badly things were going, how there was just no way that I could write.

Today, I write these words out at our farm a county north of town, a second residence my teaching money has made possible. It's a beautiful April day, a match for the early spring of three decades ago, and on our 1854 stone farmhouse's warm patio I can soak up the sun as I sip coffee from a University of Wisconsin mug that sports a lovely black ink sketch of Bascom Hall. Windows of the old speech department offices are visible, and I can think back to the little drama that was played out there so long ago, when I thought it was the last act of my academic career rather than the first. Thanking my wife's friends for the coffee and encouragement, I headed back to the English department in the opposite wing, slipping into the exam room. I looked at the test again and felt miserable. Picking up a pen was worse, for two long mornings of handwriting had

worn my fingers nearly raw. Yet physical pain could not distract me from the mental anguish, which told me it was foolish to even consider writing this exam.

Knowing full well what my decision would cost me, I gathered up pens, bluebooks, and the test paper and strode back to the graduate office. Less than an hour before, the secretary had given me the question; now, when I should have been one-third done with the answer, she was surprised to see me again, my bluebook package not even unsealed. In half a lifetime of forgotten names, I can remember hers clearly: Bev Bednar, with whom I'd dealt only three or four times before. As I said, she looked surprised when I entered but registered grave alarm as I gave her the news.

"There's no way I can take this test," I told her, handing it back as pristinely as when she'd given it to me last hour.

"Are you sick?" she asked, genuinely concerned, implying that there were procedures for dealing with this.

No, but the question is, I wanted to say but didn't. Why make her feel bad. I hated people, especially pompous academics, who took everything out on the secretaries—and not just because I was married to one.

"No, I just can't answer the question," I explained.

"Didn't you try?" she asked, looking sad. This made me feel worse.

"I've mulled it over for an hour," I told her, "but it's just not going to work. So here," I gestured, urging her to take back the paper sitting on her desk.

"You really should do something," she urged, thinking when I wasn't.

"I really can't," I quavered, wondering if I was going to break down entirely.

"Well, at least write your name on it and say you cannot answer." She looked so forlorn yet insistent that I gathered my doing this would make things easier for her, so I did. Thanking her for her help, I told her not to worry.

Hurrying out the back door of Bascom to where my bike was chained, I entered the brilliant April sunlight and suddenly felt wonderful, better than I had in months. I was free of what had been torturing me, and if that meant being free of the profession of English, then so be it—who wanted an entire life of this? Cycling home, I felt like singing, and it was probably this exuberance that helped my wife accept what was in fact a rather grim situation— but not that grim. Screw the doctorate. Even as an instructor at Northern Illinois University, I'd have eight grand a year for three years guaranteed and probably another three renewed—several

thousand more than we'd been earning combined. After that, I could teach junior college or high school or do something else entirely. When we'd met at age sixteen, my plans had been to skip college completely and manage a loan office as my aunt did. Anything was possible. The best thing was I wouldn't have to think about it until I was thirty.

Out came the stroller for another arboretum walk and picnic with our baby son. That afternoon, I stayed outside, cleaning up the yard. For dinner, we grilled steaks, a special treat, with prime beef from the boutiquelike specialty grocery store that served ritzy Nakoma. Then, after dinner when it was too dark to sit outside, I was bowled over by the day's biggest surprise. Grabbing another beer from the six-pack, I ambled into the study and with the most comfortable feeling imaginable picked up a minor Melville novel and began to read.

That was how the next half dozen weeks passed: walking the arboretum, biking around Nakoma, enjoying the great weather, and having a fine time reading odds and ends by classic authors I'd only crammed in outline form before. This was a great life, I thought: pick up my monthly fellowship check still coming in its dumb regularity from the bursar's window at school, enjoy Madison's loveliest spring in years, read all I wanted of Hawthorne, Melville, and Twain. For obvious reasons, I stayed clear of Bascom Hall, but elsewhere on campus we enjoyed Picnic Point reaching far out into Lake Mendota, fresh ice cream at the College of Agriculture's Babcock Hall, the sun-splashed Union terrace on the lakeside, and the Indian mounds on the crest of Observatory Hill.

Sometime toward the end of May, a formal-looking letter arrived from the English department. Well, here it was: my walking papers, saying I'd flunked out. Sayanora, have a nice life, and thanks for the memories— please turn out the lights as you leave. I let it sit unopened until Elaine coaxed me into taking a look; I wasn't afraid, but who cared? I'd accepted the decision six weeks ago and felt absolutely wonderful ever since.

But guess what? Unfolding the letterhead stationery, the same had been used to announce my assistantship two years ago and my fellowship a year later, I read some unbelievable news. Congratulations, it said, on passing my first two doctoral exams in eighteenth- and nineteenth-century American literature; I would be advanced to candidacy upon the successful retaking of the third, in twentieth-century American literature, to be scheduled in August.

In the moment it took to digest these lines, I was reborn. The two suc-

cesses floored me, but in the same instant, I was convinced that I had *passed,* as in a rite of passage. Perhaps I'd known that all along, as signaled by the past six weeks' serenity. Retaking just one would be a snap. If necessary, I could use summer afternoons to gear up on poststructuralism, J. D. Watson, and all that other *New York Review of Books* Anglo-kosher nonsense. But evenings would remain relaxed, while the *presto* of the morning promised something else. Reviving my original plan, I determined to get my dissertation done during June and July so that I'd start off September as a fully paid tenure-track assistant professor.

So here I was, plunged back into the stream—but with some key differences. While always applying myself to the task, it would be at a pace I determined, not others. My work with modern literature would be in the manner enjoyed over this past month and a half, since 90 percent of what I'd crammed and jammed and hystericized between January and April hadn't made it onto the exams anyway. What I did write had been learned long before, so my frenzied preparation had been for nothing. I'd pursue this style in both research and teaching, I vowed, together with a very specific pledge: never, no matter what kind of course I taught, would there be any exam—not even a pop quiz, let alone a comprehensive final. There had to be better ways of finding out what my students knew. Exams only showed what they didn't know or couldn't remember or in the moment's stress were unable to put down coherently.

After a Memorial Day weekend spent celebrating with our families back in Milwaukee, Elaine and I started off June 1 with a steady but pleasant discipline. Because I wanted August free for relaxation before the last exam, the dissertation would have to be done in two months—better yet, six weeks so that the end of July could be used for reviewing what I knew about the moderns. The quickest anyone had managed was a year; two years was the average, and some candidates let it drag on for five or six years or a lifetime. Compounding the problem was that Harry Hayden Clark, old fashioned as he was, didn't believe in the newfangled idea of hundred-page theses. The minimum he'd accept was three hundred pages. Down in the library basement in the Cutter/Tank shelving were plenty of examples, some of them running two or three volumes. I took down the longest, a nine-hundred-page study of pageantry in Hawthorne, and grasped the method at once. There was no argument to make or insight to display— just page after page dutifully listing each example of pageantry in Nathaniel Hawthorne's canon. It was disguised as a critical narrative, but even that

was a transparent device for generating such an immense page count. A quote from one of the stories or novels about pageantry would be cited in full and then restated in the dissertation writer's own more gregarious style, with the advice that this was one more example of pageantry. Each example took several pages to deal with, and there were hundreds of examples. Mr. Clark's length requirement took care of itself. Three hundred pages would be a snap.

As always, summer in Madison was great. For our first year, we'd moved into our rented house at the start of June and did nothing but relax for three months, Elaine's job hunting on hold until school started in September. Friends said it made us look years younger. The second summer, I didn't do any credit work (or pay tuition!), just sitting in on John Lyons's contemp fiction course. Now, for the summer of 1969, we had to be more serious, but the pace was our own and set toward our goals and not somebody else's.

My preparation for the twentieth-century exam was leisurely: no cram books and no attempt to read scores of modern novels. Instead, I picked out what the critics said to be best and read them for their own sense of narrative. From Lionel Trilling and Irving Howe to Frederick Hoffman, Marcus Klein, and Ihab Hassan, I ambled through chapters as if they were episodes in an adventure saga. On a whim, I ordered a copy of Robert Scholes's *The Fabulators,* not from the university bookstore but from the funky Mifflin Street Co-Op (one of the first stores in America to begin mixing literature with grocery staples), and was enchanted with the volume's concision and lucid approach. Rather than stocking up on details, I was looking for the comfort, confidence, and command of an overview. Because studying this way went so much easier—actually nothing more than leisure reading in the warm summer evenings—I trusted that this method would work.

The more strenuous task was writing the dissertation. By all rights, Mr. Clark should not have let me start until I'd passed the last exam, but in his charming confusion and unquestionable eminence he let the matter pass unnoticed. He knew I had a job starting in September and was proud that his student was one of the few with tenure-track employment in hand, so that was where he was focused: on getting me through. For my part, it meant sticking to a schedule. I figured I could get the research done in three weeks and did, running through the library's shelving and bolting stairs up the ten-stack levels rather than wait for the tediously slow elevator. Mornings I'd pillage the books and bound periodicals. Afternoons I'd type refer-

ences on large six-by-eight-inch cards. Evenings I'd sit back and enjoy the critical stories being spun by Fred Hoffman, Bob Scholes, and Ihab Hassan.

With June coming to an end, I was ready to write. Again I figured another three weeks would do the trick. Three hundred pages? That was not the way to think. No one can sit down and write three hundred pages, and thinking that one must inhibits progress or stops it cold. But anyone can write a single page, especially when the content is all prepared and an hour's time provided. There were fifteen waking hours in the day even after breaks for eating, so why not make the clock work for me and write fifteen pages per day? In three weeks, I'd have my length requirement satisfied, with nearly a month for Mr. Clark to read it and for me to rest up for the last exam. The schedule worked because the calendar did, tied as I was to the notion that each day meant a finite, measurable, and above all manageable chunk was done. I'd start right after breakfast and would usually have my fifteen pages done by late afternoon. A few times, I'd hit rough spots and struggle into the evening; once, in despair of making sense of Hawthorne's *The Marble Faun,* I pounded away through the night and did not reach my quota 'til daybreak, at which point I dropped into bed for a couple hours' sleep and then got right back to the typewriter. More often, I'd find easy stretches that let me sail past the limit and pile up pages ahead. These could be banked for future rewards; midway through, I was thirty pages in excess, which let us take off for a happy weekend in Milwaukee. As I finished each chapter on the Royal portable, Elaine would type a clean copy on bond using the Olympia office electric we'd bought for the purpose. These pages I'd deliver to Mr. Clark. Because it was summer, and neither of us had duties at school, I'd carry chapters the few blocks over to his home in Nakoma. Again, his amiable confusion never prompted him to ask how a penniless grad student could live within walking distance of such a prestigious address rather than down in the ghetto of Miffland. But for what counted, Mr. Clark was on the ball: in an age when horror stories abounded about dissertation chapters being held for months and months, my director returned each one promptly, in just a day or two, albeit with suggestions and corrections filling the margins. These Elaine retyped onto acid-free eighty-pound bond paper, two reams of which were our biggest continuing expense. But thanks to Mr. Clark's attention, they were ready for the committee and the library come September.

In three weeks, I had 315 pages, not having the nerve to stop at page 300 but unwilling to prolong things beyond my twenty-one days. Like most other lessons learned during this time, it stayed with me for life. To

this day, when I start a book, I say I'll do 2 or sometimes 3 pages a day; thus, where others would balk at the prospect of never finishing, I'd know that in three or four months, the steady march of time will guarantee me a completed typescript. It's a matter of common sense, based on a simple look around. Carpenters building houses, masons laying up a wall, farmers plowing a field, whatever—none of them was approaching his or her job as do too many English professors, sitting there and staring at the daunting prospect of having to do 300 pages (instead of just 1, 2, or 3), working when they do in fits and starts, rewriting everything that does get done, and letting concentration-shattering matters intervene. Why not just get up, leave the phone turned off, and write the damned page or pages first thing in the morning over prebreakfast coffee? If there are other duties, set the alarm an hour earlier, but get that page done. Anyone anywhere, no matter how busy, can steal a few dozen minutes to write a single page. Just do it every day, and by year's end, you'll have a book.

With a couple weeks to rest up before it, the twentieth-century American literature exam seemed less daunting. While the area committee surely wouldn't repeat that *Double Helix* question, I nevertheless took note of enough contemporary theory to be able to turn answers my way. My other shift in strategy was mechanical. Three and a half months later, my fingers were still sore from all that bluebook writing, so I decided to haul our massive Olympia office electric down to Bascom Hall and type the stuff, fluid as I'd become after banging out 315 pages on Hawthorne. The powerful machine certainly made me feel confident enough. *The Significance of the Ending to "The House of the Seven Gables"* had been no small achievement: eighty thousand words on the last paragraph of a novel! Of course, I'd found that significance to lie in how this widely criticized ending departs from the author's more successful mode of closure (where positives fail to win out over negatives), so to make my case complete I'd had to consider the complications and resolutions in the other novels and unfinished romances. A year later, I'd publish a précis of all this as a simple, straightforward essay, "Hawthorne's Sense of an Ending." An essay was just about what my arguments were worth. But in the parody of Germanic scholarship that a Ph.D. in English was (and in many cases still remains), my dissertation made me feel capable of writing on just about anything at any length needed, which positioned me much better for the retaking of this exam.

Test day was in early August, and I recall feeling exceptionally happy that there was just one. I lugged the typewriter down to the conference

room, made sure the electrical hookup was live (this was, after all, Bascom Hall, built in 1859 and only minimally improved since, to its lasting charm), then reported to the English graduate office for my test paper. Bev Bednar handed it to me with a big smile. I guessed this was self-congratulatory on getting me to cover my ass first time through—since getting the happy news in May, I'd thanked her half a dozen times. But as I returned to my typewriter, a look inside the envelope told me what had prompted her grin. Here was what she'd been instructed to type up for me: "Construct a model syllabus for a twentieth-century American literature course, offering a detailed rationale for each text chosen."

What a bunch of wimps! I almost risked saying but was so overjoyed at the summer examiners' simplicity and fairness that I could only feel generous. Okay, they'd pegged me as a teacher, not a jet-age critic; those space travelers who'd written the spring exam were surely off to conferences in beauty spots around the world just now, while my examiners were the old horses stuck here teaching summer school. But it also occurred to me that I could have caused a minor scandal by walking out on that earlier test. After all, I was the only university fellow in the department and one of just eight in the entire graduate school. Plus I had the job, publications, top grades . . . But rather than sit there and congratulate myself, I had better start writing, start typing, so I promptly spun out a convincing essay in the manner of all those Frederick Hoffman/Ihab Hassan/Robert Scholes books I'd been reading so pleasurably on summer nights since June.

Four hours later, having had plenty of time to consider everything I was saying, I turned it in and wrestled my heavy, bulky, but all-powerful typewriter down the back of Bascom Hill to where I was parked. Our little sea blue Volkswagen sagged as I eased the machine's weight onto the passenger seat, but it was a soaring ride I took home, sunroof open to the hot weather and taking corners as if I were in a Maserati. There would be no six-week wait this time, for summer results came quicker, plus mine were being expedited so that my dissertation could be officially considered. Mr. Clark had asked his colleagues Merton Sealts and William Lenehan to drop custom by reading it during their August break. Even more unusual was Stan Henning, who directed the graduate program in English, letting this committee meet in the first week of September, before the university was officially in session, to hear my defense and hopefully accept the dissertation before Northern Illinois University's first day of class. A fine point of timing, it would mean I'd start their academic year on track as an assistant professor, accruing two extra semesters of service toward tenure. So

all the dominoes were lined up. I felt confident that this morning's exam paper had sent them all falling in line.

Results were announced in a week, by phone with letter to follow. I'd passed the test and was now "advanced to candidacy," meaning I could now "begin work on my dissertation." This meant calling Mr. Clark at home and asking if I could walk over with my three sets of 315 neatly boxed pages. "Yes, yes, yes," he stammered, his slightly stumbling speech as predictable as his ready assent. But wouldn't I prefer to stop by early this evening for coffee or a brandy cordial to be shared with our wives? Well, that was wonderful, but we had our six-month-old son and no last-minute babysitter. "Oh, br-br-bring the baby along," my director urged. "We love babies, our little grandchildren visit here all the time." So with Elaine carrying Jonathan and me cradling the Hawthorne study, we strolled over to Seneca Place at 7:30 as invited.

Here it was, a warm August evening with school not in session, but Mr. Clark was dressed as always in his long-sleeved white shirt, starched collar, knotted tie, and suit pants. Mrs. Clark was only slightly less formally attired. But their manners were warmly welcoming, and within minutes the legendary Americanist scholar was down on the floor playing with our son, eliciting giggles and glee with every grandfatherly trick in the book.

From all that happened during our visit, I was impressed, but it was Elaine who seemed truly bowled over. Not that she was ever mystified by the professorate, having swept their droppings for so many years. Rather, it was the contrast between Harry Hayden Clark's immense professional power and his homely, offhand way of exercising it. The sight of him crawling around the floor with little Jonathan was part of it, but it was also the small talk about some of his old students I'd had as profs at Marquette. He mentioned one of them, the dullest, and regretted that as a UW grad the man never had made an impact. "P-p-perhaps we should arrange a Fulbright appointment for him," Mr. Clark ventured; "may-may-maybe that would help." Elaine's glance told me what she was thinking: My God, this is how things are done! A moment later, he was doing it for me, getting up from the floor and toddling off to his study so he could write a letter to my new boss at Northern Illinois saying my degree was assured, that no dissertation committee he chaired had ever done anything but vote unanimously for his candidate. The letter's form was a mess, with mistakes X'd out, margins ragged both left and right, signature scribbled like a third-grader's. But these were signs of the man's power, Elaine later assured me—the greater his clout, the more insouciant would be its expression. I never

checked back to see if Dr. Schieber got his Fulbright year away from Marquette, but I sure got my assistant professorship and extra two thousand dollars of salary.

On September 1, 1969, we left Madison for DeKalb, Illinois, just a couple hours south but a world away from where we'd so loved living. A student from one of my two semesters of teaching, Pat Quinn, helped us move, together with my TA colleague Paul Schneider. They drove the rental truck, helped us unpack, shared a big pizza with a liter of Chianti wine, then headed back to Madison. Though feeling quite desolate when they left, the break from Madison wasn't yet complete. For one thing, it was hard to accept the reality of living in DeKalb. The town's tight housing market had put us in a two-bedroom "garden" apartment in a ghastly modern complex that seemed all plywood and cheap shag carpeting. Moreover, I still had a matter of business that tied me more to UW than to NIU: my dissertation defense. It happened on September 9, the same presemester day Northern Illinois was having its general faculty meeting at which new staff would be introduced. The latter session was at the honored meeting time of all universities, 3:00 P.M., and as my defense was at 10:00 A.M. in Madison, I was able to fulfill both obligations. Had I somehow failed the defense, it would have been an exceedingly public humiliation to be introduced by NIU's president as an assistant professor knowing that such rank would be cut to instructor the next morning. But travel time was a much greater concern; when leaving DeKalb at dawn, I had to wipe morning dew from our car and then balance a coffee cup in my lap through the gear changes until I was barreling up Route 47 toward Wisconsin.

Scheduled to run ninety minutes, the defense would leave me time to deposit my thesis (with the committee's signature page) at the library, grab a burger for lunch, and hightail it back to DeKalb for the start of professorial duties. What a freshly minted Ph.D. I'd be, the three and a half hours' gap between passing a defense and assuming rank being another world's record. But luck and good timing had been my strong points all along, so I really wasn't worried.

Everything went well 'til the very end. After an hour and a half of genial, collegial talk about Hawthorne and the issues I'd raised, it looked like all was done. Mr. Clark suggested that I leave the room for a moment while the committee voted, at which point Mr. Sealts interrupted with what he said were "a few minor points." Nothing serious, just some typos to correct before the thesis went into Wisconsin's library and the ongoing history of American literary scholarship.

Typos?! Elaine and I had proofed these pages repeatedly. But Mr. Sealts raised a technicality: in subsequent abbreviated references to previously cited materials, I'd used "pp." for books but indicated just numbers for volumed journals. That was right the first time but not afterwards for essays where the volume number was no longer present: it should be "pp. 15–16," not "15–16" as I had it. Lord, that would mean retyping perhaps two hundred pages! I said it would be taken care of, meaning I'd take care of it by ignoring the problem. A year's service credit and two thousand dollars in salary were too much to sacrifice—better to make the "pp." distinction twice next time. Besides, Mr. Clark didn't seem to care, and he'd be the only committee member to have a copy. But Merton Sealts did have another point that could not be ignored: in the dissertation's very first sentence, I'd neglected to underline the title of Hawthorne's novel being studied.

Everything now became vaudeville, a slapstick scene only my haste kept me from laughing at. I stepped out into the hall, not to wonder how the committee would vote but to guess where I could find a pen and some India ink to do the underlining. When at 11:35 Mr. Clark opened the door, smiled, and extended his hand in congratulations—"Congratulations, Dr. Kl-kl-klinkowitz!"—I missed the courtesy entirely for worry about the clock. The library's thesis office closed for lunch in twenty-five minutes, and by the time it would reopen, I had to be halfway to DeKalb. Thankfully, the niceties didn't drag on, and by quarter to noon I was in Bev Bednar's office begging for ink. She had some and did the underlining herself. Before I could say thanks, she sped me off to the library, a mad dash down Bascom Hill and across the library plaza already filled with Frisbee tossers. I made it with six minutes to spare. Then it was into the car, a quick stop at the Laurel Tavern for a bag of cheeseburgers and a styrofoam coffee, and off across the kettle moraine that too soon became the flat desolation of northern Illinois.

As I write these pages this May morning, I'm back in Madison, staying in what's become a bed-and-breakfast place just two blocks over from our old Briar Hill Road home and working this morning in the former Graduate Reading Room of the library, four tall stories over Langdon Street. The official copy of my dissertation is before me, retrieved from the Cutter/Tank shelving where I found it with the other hundred-plus theses Mr. Clark directed during his four decades at UW. Elsewhere in the library are thirty-two of the three dozen books I've published to date, and an anonymous check with acquisitions tells me that three more I'm publishing this year are on order. Yet the dissertation seems most important, and not the

least because of its last page, something the library office took from my files to signify the true sense of an ending: an outline of my education going all the way back to grade school, starting in 1950. Believe it or not, first grade had been spent in one of eight rows in an honest-to-goodness one-room school house, a survivor from our suburb's rural past. Each year new classrooms, then new wings, and finally new buildings were added as the population grew, until by the time I left for high school, it was quite a complex. What an era my education had spanned. And on September 9, 1969, it was over. Dashing from the library that day, I had jumped into my VW as a harried graduate student—doctoral congratulations be damned, for there I sat, still fudging requirements and blowing town with those improper footnotes never to be corrected. But in the two-hour drive that followed, something changed. Pulling into NIU's faculty parking lot, I felt I belonged there, and as I walked into the huge meeting room, I felt I belonged there, too. Even though so many of us had been newly hired that our introductions were less than ten seconds each, I had more than my necessary quota of fame. I was in; I had made it, just when times had changed and such success was said to be impossible. By all accounts and measures, I shouldn't be here. But here I was.

2
Home Schooling

At Marquette, I'd taught three semesters of quiz sections in the English lit survey, while my single year's TA work at Wisconsin had been in composition, according to a strictly followed syllabus. It was only at Northern Illinois that I had any control over what I was teaching and how. My section of comp still seemed pointless in that we had no real texts for reference, just essays whose form got obliterated by controversies of content—sure, students will read an article for or against abortion, but how do you direct discussion to style when some of them might be pregnant themselves? During this first of my years at NIU, my old grad student colleagues back in Madison felt the same way and lobbied for the right to include a novel or story collection in their comp sections so that at least they'd have an analyzable piece of good writing to teach. When argument and persuasion (which they'd been trying to teach) failed to impress the administration, they unionized and struck. Because their representation was the Teamsters, their act halted all deliveries and closed the campus for a week.

How the UW English department leadership responded did more to change composition in the curriculum than anything the TAs could have done. What the department did was drop it! For years, the administration had insisted a writing course was absolutely necessary for students, but once the issue became one of even partial autonomy for writing teachers, the subject disappeared from Wisconsin's course catalog. Suddenly, many members of the newly formed Teaching Assistants Association were out of work, for the curricular replacement left far fewer sections to staff. If you didn't have a research assistantship or a graduate fellowship, better find a job at McDonald's—a job with lots of overtime, because you were losing your out-of-state tuition waiver, too. Thirty years later, the Graduate Program in English had not fully recovered from this general slaughter, but at least the department leaders "felt right" about things. Maybe those radical TAs

who'd shocked me earlier by equating our professors with Pentagon war-lords were right after all, as scorched earth was all that was left in the free-fire zone of what had once been a top-rated program.

The situation at Northern Illinois was far from being so politicized. After this first semester, I was never asked to teach writing again, and even now was having my load balanced by two sections of an advanced course in American realism and naturalism. I'd never had an American lit survey course and only absorbed the Brit lit cycle as a quiz-section TA, so creating a context was my first piece of home schooling. It came from the generalist reading I'd done for my comprehensive exams and consisted not so much of the period definitions as of the transitions from one to another. Central to these passages were shifting emphases between the metaphysical and the material, less of a strict alternation than a progression always searching for resolution but never finding it. Beginning this first semester and continuing for as long as I'd teach American literature, I'd start off with a day or two's discussion of this outline, placing the course's period within the larger framework and considering how it fit. For each era, the shift from the spiritual to the social or vice-versa was for a different reason, and in that difference lay the essence of what we were studying. With that much out of the way, we were free to concentrate on just what was happening in each text we read. History was important but not distracting, for we already knew where it all was heading (instead of reinventing the drive wheel for each successive piece of writing).

The other important feature I emphasized was also related to transitions, specifically what we were experiencing when we finished one author's text and moved on to another's. It was something that hadn't been exploited in so much of my own course work. As a philosophy minor at Marquette, I'd noticed how when we studied Kant, we were all Kantians and then promptly started thinking like Hegel when the course proceeded to him. My lit classes at both Marquette and Wisconsin were done the same way, even to the point that during the contemp fiction course Mr. Lyons would look and act and sound like Asa Leventhal as we studied Bellow's *The Victim* but then become Rabbit Angstrom when we moved on to Updike. At no point was I encouraged to consider the gap between. It was a gap: that was the point. Kant's idealism had been reversed, Bellow's deep moralism given a polish of good (and bad) manners. But as for what was in between, that was something that didn't exist or didn't count. But now, in my first semester of genuine teaching, it became evident that what lay in between was my own experience of reading.

specialty, Hawthorne and the romantics, it would have been hard enough. But as the most junior of faculty members, there was another hard duty awaiting me: not just another first-hour class but one in the twentieth-century American novel to boot. Had Arnold Fox, who scheduled courses and found out by now I wasn't the nice young Jewish boy he'd intended to recruit, discovered this was my weakest area, that I'd failed my doctoral exam on it by walking out and almost ending my academic career right there? Did he think I'd quit again now? True, I'd finally passed the twentieth-century exam, but only when being served up an obvious sweetheart pitch, a batting practice fastball even my grandmother could have hit. The harder question now was whether or not I could teach this stuff.

Hemingway-Fitzgerald-Faulkner would be easy enough, as I'd read most of their books on my own, plus John Lyons' course had me at least superficially familiar with the next batch, Updike-Bellow-Malamud. Because I wanted my own course to be more contemporary than the end-it-at-1948 classes I'd taken at Marquette, I resolved to include somebody current and was pleased to learn that the previously unknown paperbacker I'd been reading for fun, Kurt Vonnegut, had in the past six months become famous. Back in April, during the same week I'd been sweating my doctoral comps, he had published his sixth novel, which after twenty years of writing became his first best seller, *Slaughterhouse-Five*. This had brought his earlier works back into print, readily available in cheap editions for easy teaching. Not that students needed a curriculum to read him. Instead, in the spirit of self-directed learning that characterized the new era, Vonnegut (along with Ken Kesey, Joseph Heller, Richard Brautigan, and a few others) had become part of a canon that young people formed for themselves. This meant digging up books going back to the earlier sixties and even fifties. But the effort also created a new literary tradition, a self-proclaimed alternative stream in which new writers such as Tom Robbins, William Kotzwinkle, Rob Swigart, and Gerald Rosen would flourish.

If the kids could do this, so could young assistant professors, and in choosing Kurt Vonnegut to end my course, I was joining ranks with colleagues elsewhere who were establishing a new pedagogical style: trimming away redundantly modern or manneristic works to make room for others who had set off in a new direction. Vonnegut was an obvious example, as were Kesey and Heller. More adventurous choices were Donald Barthelme, Grace Paley, Ronald Sukenick, and Ishmael Reed, all of whom had their followings. The helpful nature of Vonnegut's work was that it had com-

mon sources in both the old and new streams; he was a unique example of how radical students and experimenting teachers could meet on level ground. From the teacher's side, the change was obvious. There were no imposing texts being handed down from Olympus, as it were, trailing clouds of mandatory glory. Instead, works by Vonnegut met us as equals, with a new literary world to be created right here and now. There was no accepted meaning, nothing to be authoritatively imposed. Indeed, none of us, neither teacher nor student, was sure just what Vonnegut's fiction meant. Understanding had to be created, and we'd have to do it together.

People talk about the sixties in terms of academic change, but the real transformation began in the spring of 1970, when all that had been happening in the last few years came crashing down into otherwise normal lives. Demonstrations that once seemed abstract exercises now felt more like total war. Tempers on both sides were frayed by such pressures. No more flowers in gun barrels—brickbats and fire bombs were more the style, and by May the guns were fired in anger. Northern Illinois University suffered nothing like Kent State and Jackson State, but our campus was occupied by the Illinois National Guard, loaded guns and all. As the semester drew into its final weeks, I was spending nights watching combat-outfitted squads and state police in riot gear flush out resisters, while in daylight hours I continued searching for a way to teach Vonnegut's *Mother Night,* the novel I'd chosen to end things. To this day, I can't read Kurt's novel, set as it is in a police state during our century's most volatile years, without recalling the smell of tear gas and sounds of sirens and bullhorns echoing all night long that characterized our own much milder disruption.

Mother Night fit in no better with what I had been teaching than those improbable commando squads and SWAT teams fit the campus landscape. Here was where my cyclic sense of progression broke down. Even the term *modern* had a time peg to it, while *contemporary* meant "right now." What would we call Vonnegut and his style thirty years from now? I knew the term *postmodern* but didn't like it. It said nothing positive (I *had* learned something from Harry Hayden Clark!), and I despaired of dealing with a literature that dealt only with negatives (as the books by Barth and Pynchon touted by Madison's *Contemporary Literature* crowd seemed to do). Plenty of critics were working on contemp lit, but by that they meant people like Norman Mailer (a bestseller in 1948) and Saul Bellow (whose first novel appeared in 1944). In time, I'd come up with the term *postcontemporary* as a way of signaling both a literature and a style of criticism without pre-

conceived interpretation. It was by addressing such works that my own generation of critics and teachers so naturally fell into step with what literary theorists called "postmodernism" and "deconstruction." To begin with, there was not a lot we knew about Vonnegut, but from seeing all the premises he questioned, it was pretty clear what he wasn't. Although his texts came to us virtually naked, we didn't study them in isolation. Nor did we use his independence to parody New Critical technique, which quite obviously didn't focus on the work itself (as claimed) but in fact carried with it a healthy dose of humanism. Where Kurt Vonnegut came from was evident: his last three books contained autobiographical prefaces, and even within the fictive texts we could see evidence of growing up in the Great Depression and serving in World War II. But this author's social conscience wasn't John Steinbeck's, nor were his soldiers fit for a Hemingway, Mailer, or even James Jones novel. Though he was old enough to have done so, Kurt Vonnegut could never have written *Mother Night* or *Slaughterhouse-Five* in the forties. Their subject was the 1939–1945 war, but their tone, texture, and meaning were necessarily of the sixties, an era that had evolved before our eyes and without help just as our educations had been concluding. Here was where home schooling could begin, as all of us tried to figure out the literature so genuinely of our times.

Most apparent was that the cycle of American literature, at least in terms of its handiness for teaching, had been disrupted. For three hundred years, there had been an obvious thesis/antithesis between spiritual and material, metaphysical and physical, divine and mundane, ideal and real, individual and social that defined one period's distinction from another. By 1920, modernism had knocked that predictable spiral off course in favor of what its practitioners claimed at the time was a final synthesis. But when modernism began to falter as a sustainable world view, the nature of its deconstruction revealed not just that one era's thinking was coming apart but that an entire intellectual and aesthetic culture was being questioned and found no longer adequate to needs.

The beauty of Kurt Vonnegut's work was that it undertook such challenges from a very familiar viewpoint: not of the arty, brainy avant-garde (which if pursued would have yielded just a "more modern modern," as French critics called it) but of the homely perspective of the American middle class. Here the art was popular and the thought decidedly lowbrow, making Vonnegut's integration of the two sound a lot more like that of a stand-up comic from Indiana than that of a Parisian philosopher or New

York intellectual. The man's most frequently cited influence was that of the great film and radio comedians of the thirties, figures who provided the attitudes underlying his family magazine stories of the fifties, a writing experience that further strengthened the commonality of his fiction of the sixties. Vonnegut's method in the novel, like mine in class, was inductive—of the plain old English variety, so different from the deductive ratiocination polluting current academic thought.

All of this helped me prepare for teaching *Mother Night,* and when the week for it turned out to be right in the middle of the Kent State troubles, our own reactions became part of the course. After all, if everything happening in the streets was not a genuine popular response to the government's policies, what was? In more peaceful times, Vonnegut's satire of Hitler, Roosevelt, Nazi Germany, contemporary Israel, the Soviet Union, and all else in the spectrum might have seemed an academic exercise. Kent State and Vietnam made it real, and in the author's response to Nazism and World War II we found analogies for our own feelings. Old enough to be our father or not, Kurt Vonnegut had become popular only with our generation's reading.

Because we took Vonnegut in his context and at his word, my students and I avoided the modernist pitfall of thinking he was a nihilist. Only when he was perceived in terms of another era could his work be seen as anything but hopeful. If life does indeed seem without purpose, perhaps it is because humankind has tried (and failed!) to impose a purpose beyond all appropriate measures. The quest for meaning, especially as pursued by the high moderns, can be self-defeating; what else can be expected when one is guided so rigidly by conventions that no longer apply? Kurt Vonnegut's propositions only seem radical because those outdated modernist conventions persist, thanks in large part to the sloth of teachers and critics unwilling to look around them and see what's happening.

It helped that Vonnegut's work was being created out of our own conditions. As our class studied *Mother Night,* he himself was drafting his commencement address for Bennington College, a piece subsequently published in *Vogue* and collected as part of *Wampeters, Foma and Granfalloons.* Yet neither was he living in a traditionless vacuum of the purely current. He had read the same authors we did, including Melville and Thoreau. "Call me Jonah—my parents almost did" are the words that open *Cat's Cradle,* while the stories of *Welcome to the Monkey House* are prefaced with this disclaimer: "Beware of all enterprises that require new clothes." In his

commentaries on public issues of the day, he almost always went back to America's culture during the Great Depression and World War II in order to make his point about just how traditional and basically American pacifism and dissent were. Unlike the black humorists with whom he was too easily linked—Terry Southern, J. P. Donleavy, Bruce Jay Friedman—Kurt Vonnegut was writing quite consciously within the American canon, even if it didn't want to accept him just yet. So that was how we studied him: as an outsider perfectly understandable on his own terms but with plenty to offer within any construct made from what we knew.

The second contemporary introduced to my teaching was Ronald Sukenick, and similar relationships guided this choice as well. My experience teaching *Mother Night* had convinced me that one couldn't extend a course into the present day by picking some new book at random. It had to fit in somehow with what we had been reading, even if the essence of that fit meant turning the couplings inside out. For "out" to mean anything at all, it had to relate to the "in," and discussing such relationships was how my students and I made sense of the apparently absurdist text Vonnegut had produced. Sukenick's *Up,* which I'd picked out of a Dell college catalog the following fall, was an even more radical piece of work. But as with Vonnegut's fiction, there was a link. Name recognition had drawn me to Sukenick's novel, for its author was the scholar whose *Wallace Stevens: Musing the Obscure* I'd read in preparation for my last doctoral exam. Might there be an explication for Sukenick's own artistic method in this book on his favorite poet? It was worth checking out.

Aligning Vonnegut and Sukenick was the act that made both interpretation and literary history clear, and it was an act that was first of all pedagogical. Criticism and scholarly research followed, but it was having to deal with these materials in the classroom that got my career going. When it came to handling an established subject, I found it easy to rely on notes from graduate courses and my own preparation for comps. Publications, that other professional requirement, were also redundant: anything I had to say on Hawthorne, Howells, and Faulkner, for example, would make for just a timid half-step within established boundaries. But with truly contemporary texts, there were no fixed limits, just a grounding from which these writers had taken their last step. Having mastered that ground, why not follow along? The key was figuring out what they were doing without being overly prejudiced about where you thought they should go.

Vonnegut was certainly new enough, but with Sukenick being even

newer, a pattern emerged, one that proved useful for teaching. Among current innovators, there was an obvious move from simplicity to complexity, almost as if subsequent writers were taking advantage of paths cleared and new routes established by their predecessors. With John Somer, an NIU instructor just beginning doctoral work but having four textbooks to his credit already, I began hashing over this approach, until a late night party conversation turned into a Saturday's work on the table of contents for what we considered the ideal course materials. We didn't want to sum up or cover contemporary American fiction. That would be impossible, like "loading mercury with a pitchfork," as one of the writers we liked, Richard Brautigan, put it in a book title. Any attempt would turn off users who didn't find their favorite writer represented—and there were hundreds of favorites. What we sought was a method, a vehicle that would take students and other readers from what they did know well into what they didn't. True, much current lit seemed inexplicable if not downright unreadable; but we didn't want to take the easy way out and just drop that stuff. It would be in our anthology but toward the end, step ten or eleven in the process. Compared to our beginning, step one, that would be quite a gap. But no one would be going straight from one to fifteen. From one to two—from Vonnegut, say, to Hughes Rudd—would be easy, a simple expansion of the same offbeat comic vision to accommodate technique. From there, it would be a matter of a dozen more such steps through Richard Brautigan, Robert Coover, Donald Barthelme, and the like until we were poised for the leap of faith into Sukenick. As teachers, our task would be to make that leap as well prepared and as confidence building as possible.

Hughes Rudd was not an innovative avant-gardist but a CBS Television newsman, so his casual stories were a natural complement to Vonnegut's easygoing kickoff to *Innovative Fiction,* as John and I called our prospective volume. Then would come Richard Brautigan, current and radical yet with the same charming accessibility as Vonnegut and Rudd. All three writers took something basically familiar but with a sense of the fabulous to it—in Vonnegut's "The Hyannis Port Story," the glamour and mystique of the current Kennedy clan—and reshaped it into something comfortably manageable. This transformation was done by manipulating signs, which in the day's critical language was called "semiology" but for Vonnegut became as simple as an unassuming tradesman expressing his views. From here, we lined up writers who handled popular forms more roughly, but John and I sought out their stories that were accessible rather than deliberately alienating, stories that carried the students along rather than cast-

ing them off by the wayside. Coover's babysitter fraught with late-night fears, Barthelme's porcupines occupying a university campus—there was plenty here that even the least sophisticated readership could follow, still essentially innovative but so different from "The Elevator" and "Bone Bubbles," the brainier pieces by these authors more often chosen for anthologies.

The other link-up helping our book was the critical/creative one. I'd already mined Ron Sukenick's Wallace Stevens book for insights into his fiction and found this very useful one: "Adequate adjustment to the present can only be achieved through ever fresh perception of it" (3). Was contemporary realism as it was too chaotic? Well, by looking at Stevens's poetry, Ron had an answer to this one, too: "The mind orders reality not by imposing ideas on it but by discovering significant relations with it" (12). So it wasn't simple idealism, rather something more spectacular and much more in line with our times: "When, through the imagination, the ego manages to reconcile reality with its own needs, the formerly insipid landscape is infused with the ego's emotion; and reality, because it now seems intensely relevant to the ego, suddenly seems more real" (14–15). There was the term: *relevance,* our generation's catchword. And here it was applicable to innovative fiction, something the social critics considered the most irrelevant of all.

This was the framework John and I used, not just for presenting Sukenick's fiction but for explaining how all these innovators could continue to write when the world had outrun realism's ability to represent it. Appropriately, we found the words to describe this state of affairs in Ron's novella, "The Death of the Novel," as collected in *The Death of the Novel and Other Stories.* The opening paragraphs read like criticism but are in fact fiction, part of the protagonist's lecture to his creative writing class, not a theoretical dictate but (as the book's subtitle implies) just another story:

> Fiction constitutes a way of looking at the world. Therefore I will begin by considering how the world looks in what I think we may now begin to call the contemporary post-realistic novel. Realistic fiction presupposed chronological time as the medium of a plotted narrative, an irreducible individual psyche as the subject of its characterization, and, above all, the ultimate, concrete reality of things as the object and rationale of its description. In the world of post-realism, however, all of these absolutes have become absolutely problematic.
>
> The contemporary writer—the writer who is acutely in touch

with the life of which he is part—is forced to start from scratch: Reality doesn't exist, time doesn't exist, personality doesn't exist. God was the omniscient author, but he died: now no one knows the plot, and since our reality lacks the sanction of a creator, there's no guarantee as to the authenticity of the received version. Time is reduced to presence, the content of a series of discontinuous moments. Time is no longer purposive, and so there is no destiny, only chance. Reality is, simply, our experience, and objectivity is, of course, an illusion. Personality, after passing through a phase of awkward self-consciousness, has become, quite minimally, a mere locus for our experience. In view of these annihilations, it should be no surprise that literature, also, does not exist—how could it? There is only reading and writing, which are things we do, like eating and making love, to pass the time, ways of maintaining a considered boredom in the face of the abyss.

Not to mention a series of overwhelming social dislocations. (41)

Over the years, I've developed a theory that whenever an author is going to try something different from conventional expectations, he or she will teach you how to read it on the first page. Here, Ron Sukenick was doing just that. The "death of the novel" was not the final word in criticism, his novella says—it's just one account among many, any of which might prevail for a moment and only then because of its timely (and therefore passing) persuasiveness. In *The Death of the Novel and Other Stories,* it was, in fact, one of the more traditional pieces, relying as it does on a familiar expositional device: a protagonist lecturing about a literary theory that parallels the struggles in his personal and professional life.

John came up with the insight into just what Ron had accomplished. Even as the author said it was impossible for him to write and us to read, he was writing and we were reading. These were functions that had their own momentum, and it was that impulse he was capturing. His collection had a story with this very title, "Momentum," and we included it for its good example of how conventions change to accommodate this new emphasis on reality as process rather than as product. Looking back to the Wallace Stevens book, we could see just how the writer's imagination made aspects of the world more pertinent and hence more real; perhaps the reader's imagination could do something similar in relation to the text. By

locating so much of his early work in the world of college students and the equally young junior faculty teaching them, Sukenick was quite cleverly building a happy relationship with users of his books.

Robert Coover's "The Babysitter" was our next big step. It's a powerful but entertaining demonstration of how the postmodern world is indeed a construct of various, sometimes conflicting perceptions, interpretations, and sources. In formal terms alone, it could have proved unreadable, consisting as it does of disjunctive paragraphs hopscotching through an action that while basically chronological makes no distinction between what's "really" happening and what isn't. Fantasy and history intermix, all the more confusing when several people's worries, neuroses, and even psychoses are stirred in. Yet Coover holds it all together by locating his narrative within the simplest of actions, that of a teenage girl with a worrisome assignment: taking care of two incorrigible little kids, while fending off her randy boyfriend, her lustfully drunk employer, and her own dark closet of fears.

Here was the difference, I found, between truly innovative fiction and the "black humor" earlier critics presumed it to be. The latter writers—most notably Terry Southern, Bruce Jay Friedman, and Stanley Elkin—owed their notoriety to flamboyant thematics. Southern especially was a master of the *outré,* shocking readers with his egregious topics and inflammatory attitudes. Yet few of the black humorists did anything with technique. Wild as the subject matter was, their tales proceeded according to the same conventions that drove any Updike or Cheever story. Indeed, that was the essence of black humor's appeal: a deadpan progress through carnivals of the ridiculous, while never breaking the smooth stylistic surface. But John and I thought black humor was a good place to start, and there was enough of it in Rudd, Vonnegut, and Coover to let readers feel there would be some fun to be had. Rudd's fondness for Texas lore and expression carried him into innovative territory, and with Vonnegut's pop semiotics in between, Coover's fragmentation of reality as perceived could be better understood, especially once readers gathered that his text was speaking for itself. People's words, people's fears, people's thoughts, and even people's voices as broadcast on the television set the babysitter has left on are all dutifully recorded on an equal level, mocking conventional stylistics with an nonhierarchal effect of an all-over language in which the reader swims as if at sea.

Nonhierarchal, all-over—these phrases pertinent to Coover's method had been used just a decade before to describe what otherwise perplexing painters were doing. There were few represented objects in the works of Jackson Pollock, Franz Kline, and Willem de Kooning. If viewers were look-

ing to see what these paintings were "about," they'd be frustrated to find anything other than the paintings themselves. There was an echo here of modernist writing trying to escape groundings in psychology and myth in favor of going postmodern; Gertrude Stein tried it by saying that what you see is what there is, and Samuel Beckett thought it happened in Joyce's *Finnegans Wake* (to the extent that this great novel was not about something but rather was that something itself). For abstract expressionist painting, the case was more obvious, especially in Harold Rosenberg's articulation that for these action painters, the canvas was not a surface on which to represent but an arena within which to act. Were Coover and Sukenick action writers with language, just as Vonnegut and Rudd played action games with pop culture signs? It would be a good device for teaching their work, an analogy that could not be more graphic, right there in front of your eyes. A decade and half later, Ron Sukenick would confirm this truth by subtitling *In Form,* his book of critical pieces, *Digressions on the Act of Fiction*—not "art," as in Henry James, but "act."

Thanks to student involvement, I was able to begin not just working on writers but working with them. The "with" worked two ways: their texts and getting in touch with the authors themselves. Correspondence began in fall 1970, at the start of my second year as a jackleg specialist in contemp. My twentieth-century course had trimmed the moderns down to Fitzgerald, Hemingway, and Faulkner, giving the middle portion to Bellow, Malamud, and Updike, before rounding things out with three current authors. For this semester, I chose Vonnegut, Sukenick, and (for the students' sake) James S. Kunen, who as a freshman at Columbia had written *The Strawberry Statement,* a nonfiction novel about the disruptions there just a couple years before. Because Sukenick had impressed me as the most obvious of several new novelists with doctorates who were grafting critical ideas into their fiction, I wrote him at his *MLA Directory* address to let him know how I was teaching his first novel, *Up,* in the context of ideas from his Wallace Stevens book. When he answered enthusiastically, I took his letter to school, only to meet some student-generated enthusiasm. Would I mind if James S. Kunen came to class when his book was up for discussion? I thought they were joking, but in fact, a group had found Kunen's number in the Manhattan phone book and given him a call. He was more excited than they were and jumped at the chance to come speak as part of the student government's lecture series (which had hosted William Kunstler, attorney for the Chicago Eight of Democratic National Convention notoriety). Kunen would love to meet with our class as well.

Jim's visit was the first of many writers' calls, and the manner of his presence nicely demystified things before any such mystification could begin. I really do believe he was more thrilled by the event than were my students—for, after all, just two years before, he'd been no different from them. In fact, he was having no small difficulty adjusting to writerly fame. As he told us on the way in from O'Hare, where I'd taken two of the ring-leaders to pick him up (my VW bug sat only four), the sight of all those *Strawberry Statements* stacked in bookstores up and down Fifth Avenue spooked him. He'd lurk there incognito and fidget when potential read-ers handled the book and put it back down. Were they rejecting him or just the Random House product? Was it really his book at all? One day, he'd walked into Brentano's and began signing them, alarming a clerk who in a scolding way asked if he was intending to buy all these copies being appropriated with his name. When she discovered what his name was, her mood changed, and he was stuck there signing the whole table's worth while a crowd gathered, just the last thing he wanted to happen.

Indeed, the book itself had a self-effacing manner to it that we saw re-peated in Jim's behavior, all of which helped teach us how to work with his writing. Like *Slaughterhouse-Five* and *Up, The Strawberry Statement* is the story of its own making. It is not "about" the troubles at Columbia but rather details the author's struggles to write—thus making *The Straw-berry Statement* a close approximation of Gertrude Stein's and Samuel Beck-ett's protopostmodern visions, yet without the heavy baggage of high art—remember, the act of fiction, not art. There's a bit of the old student dodge here, the "I can't figure out how to answer this question" routine that in its ponderings fills the length requirement and sometimes even solves the problem. More crucial is the obvious honesty of it all, the refusal to pose and disinclination to suspend disbelief. No hierarchies, no suggestion of anything beyond what there most simply is: all of this put Jim Kunen right in there with the others we were studying, and his working with us made the experience of his writing all the more effective. A year later, the col-laboration with my class bore fruit, two baskets of it. Jim wrote the fore-word to *Innovative Fiction,* while I wrote his draft board a letter (soon pub-lished as a critical essay in the *North American Review*) supporting his conscientious objector request.

More than a quarter century after this Kunen business, the advantages of working newer writers into any lit course still hold. When the writing itself has not yet been canonized, students are less inhibited from respond-ing critically. Written in their own language and of their own times, such

works need no contextual explanations and address the reader in egalitarian rather than pontifical ways. Accessible on the page, such writers are similarly accessible in person, eager to promote their books but not yet priced out of the market like their more famous elders. They appeal to students who through their activity funds have more cash for speakers than do English departments, where faculties and administrators almost always go for the big established names—just the ones whose works intimidate students and who are more likely to give a canned speech rather than promote genuine interaction.

As John Somer and I continued with our approaches to new works, more writers made campus visits. For Jim Kunen's, I'd thrown a big party over at our rented home—no longer the "garden apartment" but now a huge Victorian house in DeKalb's hippie district, the equivalent of Madison's Miffland (which we'd shunned). Next door to the student underground newspaper and up the street from a witches' coven, our Kunen party broke the department drill by including just a few professors. When Ron Sukenick came by next year, the practice was repeated. Both times, the house was jammed with students mixing with a few instructors and new assistant profs; I kept the couple of necessary old department dogs safely kenneled in the kitchen, where a budget-busting supply of Glenlivet single-malt Scotch left them nicely self-chained.

Part of Sukenick's visit included a readers' theater presentation of his novel *Up*. I wrote the adaptation and worked with the production for six weeks, adapting lines as various blockings were tried out. Compressing a three-hundred-page novel into a one-act drama was tough, but Sukenick's broadly presentational manner made it seem natural. Plus Ron's privileging of language made the actors' voices an appropriate medium. The director was a speech department guest from Hollywood: Sydney Smith, an old character actor who knew all the tricks. Seeing him work with my students was a pleasure, and when the adaptation was presented during the Illinois Interpretation Festival coinciding with Sukenick's appearance, it pleased everyone, including Ron. Once again, my students and I were working with literature from the inside, making Ron—who watched our dress rehearsal from the empty theater's last row, sitting there like a passively observant God—feel like the characters were walking out of his head and taking on life before him.

Was it the life of fiction or the fiction of life? Or better yet, were the two reversible, one a factor in generating the other? The play, the visit (with its class meetings, play, reading, and parties), and our continuing course

work with *Up* flowed together as one experience. This was truly different from the preparations I'd worked up the first semester of my first year in that apartment study. Now, like the big old funky house we'd moved to, literature and life flowed in the doors and out the windows, filling rooms as if they were chapters in a novel. I knew the students felt this way, too, as knots of them hung on in various workshop groups that met at our home on weekday evenings and banded together for weekend trips to Chicago or the countryside in pursuit of literature in the making.

It was in this atmosphere that John and I decided to assemble our ideas for *Innovative Fiction* and send the book off to Sukenick's editor at Dell. Within a week, it was accepted, and in August of 1972 the little rack-sized paperback was out and selling for ninety-five cents. Through four printings, it would sell hundreds of thousands of copies, serving as the perfect epilogue to standard lit courses and as the basis for more thorough contemporary delvings. Even before it was out, we'd placed another project with Dell: *The Vonnegut Statement,* a group of original essays recruited and put together in the manner of our teaching. For his doctorate at NIU, John had elected to write on Kurt Vonnegut, specifically how *Slaughterhouse-Five* was the culmination of efforts over twenty years and five previous novels to express what turned out to be at heart of the matter of Dresden, where as a prisoner of war this author as a young American infantryman had seen seventy thousand civilians and the cultural treasure they were inhabiting destroyed by the modern scientific miracle of a firestorm. That in itself was part of our method, reading works not in isolation but within the context of a writer's development. In my own work, I looked at Vonnegut's short fiction, including the half of it never collected, and began using reference books to dig out the man's nonfiction, all of which offered further clues to what made his later novels so uncannily effective. We involved colleagues and students, pooling thoughts and dividing responsibilities, such as having grad students Karen and Charles Wood cover the science fiction aspects (which they'd taught as junior college instructors) and Tim Hildebrand respond as one of Vonnegut's many undergraduate readers, something I'd at first hoped Jim Kunen might do.

After three years, my patience with Northern Illinois University was wearing out. With two books in press, I was ready for a jump up, but our department had been filled pretty tightly with senior professors in the half decade preceding my arrival. I could have stayed. When the University of Northern Iowa offered me an associate professorship at half again the good salary I was earning at DeKalb, the department head pledged to match it.

But I was eager to move on, because it was as a specialist in contemp that I was being recruited, with the added lure of being able to set my own terms of employment. In addition to the two Dell anthologies appearing now, I had published critical essays on Hawthorne, Howells, Faulkner, Vonnegut, Sukenick, Kosinski, and others plus had a contracted booklength bibliography on Kurt Vonnegut ready for delivery—hence, the rank and salary. But I'd learned much about teaching while at Northern Illinois and felt even better taking this experience with me.

The first lesson had come from Arnold Fox, a Howells scholar and assistant department head whose job it was to visit each new hire's class. Seeing what I was up to that first semester back in 1969, his advice was friendly but firm: stop the deadpan lecturing, get the students to talk, and when I did want to say something do it in a conversational, interactive way. Just listening accomplished nothing. To learn, students had to make some motion themselves, engaging in a dialogue with literature, of which I was just an agent. Talk with them, not at them, Arnold counseled. By the time I was thrown into that first twentieth-century course (and had no notes!), I was ready to give the Fox method a try.

The second came in one of those same Northern Illinois classrooms, but from an off-campus visitor, Ron Sukenick. During his DeKalb stay, my other course (on realism and naturalism) was doing Frank Norris, and as Ron had the morning free, he came along. *McTeague* is a lively enough novel, and I was loaded for bear with notes on all the now-wacky scientific ideas that motivate its plot. The session went well enough, with plenty of discussion, but afterward Ron was shaking his head.

"Fifty minutes on a piece of literature," he sighed, "and not one word about language!"

What could he mean? Wasn't *McTeague* all about Lombrosian criminality, Darwinian selection, determination by class and physiognomy, and all that? Surely, this was the interesting stuff. Well, maybe Frank Norris's work was not the best place to start with attention to language. But Ron's complaint got me thinking, and I began shifting focus from that day on.

Third, and most important, was the NIU department head's idea of curriculum, less a solid pedagogy than an administrative ploy for money-making, but instructive nevertheless. Though I'd supposedly completed my academic education, here was an important professional phrase I was hearing for the first time: *generating credit hours*. Charles Hagelman had been a dean down in Texas but took a step up in coming to head NIU's English

department with its fifty full-time appointments and (for now) growing. He wanted a doctoral program and got it, realizing all those small seminars would have to be paid for with heavy enrollments elsewhere. The traditional way would be to run some mass sections of a popular course like film history, letting one prof's lectures to a roomful of five hundred pay the bills for a score of intimate grad classes. Dr. Hagelman had a better idea, part of his general philosophy of creating favorable opportunities by turning bad situations to the good. He was using this approach to generate credit hours in Texas-size numbers worthy of his fast-track University of Houston careerism, and as always, I paid attention to how he did it.

You had to be careful of these East Texas operators who had taken over NIU's English department, and by reputation Chuck Hagelman was the bull-goose operator of them all. Most of his advice was good, such as what he told me as part of his congratulations for the essays I had appearing in *Modern Fiction Studies* and *Critique* during my first year on staff: very good, but don't neglect my teaching, for it was by my students that I'd be known. A year and a half later, when I visited his office to collect kudos for placing *Innovative Fiction* and *The Vonnegut Statement* with Dell, he was all praise, with no cautions whatsoever. "That's top drawer, Jerry, absolutely top drawer!" he crowed, pleasing me no end, until a moment later when the phone rang, someone told him a broken screen had been replaced, and he replied in the same booming voice that this was "absolutely top drawer" too. He'd do things like book all fifty of us into the Midwest Modern Language Association Convention and charter a university bus to St. Louis, where we'd pile out to someone's sarcastic cheer of, "Go get 'em, Huskies!" But for piling up credit hours, his plan worked both financially and educationally. I bought into it enthusiastically in 1970 and by the end of the nineties could look back and see how it changed my entire approach to teaching literature. Indeed, the only folks who didn't like it then and now have been those who believed English departments had to be dispirited, boring, and broke.

Hagelman's plan involved creating three lower-level courses: Introduction to Fiction, Introduction to Poetry, and Introduction to Drama. Clientele would be students filling up general education hours. The courses could be staffed by any of the abundant instructors, most of whom would be grateful for relief from teaching composition and reading all those papers. These same instructors, their appetites whetted by teaching lit, could then be seduced into the department's doctoral program, the degree from

which would qualify them as literature professors forever. But regular profs would be encouraged to teach these courses, too. With complete autonomy over texts and methods, they could design classes to their special interests without having to "cover the canon" in any historical sense; the canon would be a matter of what constituted literature itself, rather than any national or historic body of work.

Objections were easy to refute. Why not just one course combining the three genres? Well, for several reasons. If given a choice, students would feel better, having less of a sense of something being shoved down their throats. All three genres together would be force-feeding at its worst, with the deception that everything about literature was being mastered; that way, attention would be diverted toward distinctions of genre rather than in understanding what literature was and how it functioned. Hagelman's three-course option avoided all this, making no grand promises and suggesting a more relaxed approach instead. What was the difference, especially to a nonmajor, between reading one genre or another if the point was not theoretical distinction but rather the skill and pleasure of responding to literary art? For the teacher, there would be no pressure to cover a supposedly complete subject (as in a hard science) but rather the admission that anything read was just an introduction to an infinity of pleasures. If you liked one, take another—take two, take three, they're small. All three were just a beginning. When happily taught, these courses would be a great advertisement for the department, where students from other disciplines might take the occasional advanced course, enriching the experience for everyone. This was far better than having the student body at large associate the English department with a bear of a composition course being taught by a misery-laden instructor slated to be fired, no matter how good he or she was, in five years or less.

It was so simple. Literature was meant for pleasure, not analysis. Analysis could be a means to that pleasure and certainly was worth the work. But it was not an end in itself. Though he was wise not to proclaim it, Charles Hagelman was admitting that as opposed to colleagues teaching physics, philosophy, or engineering, we were in the entertainment business. As such, our courses should be the most sought-after in the university, for all the right educational reasons. If we made money in the process, who could complain?

Two factors especially contributed to these courses' success: autonomy and size. Autonomy applied to both teacher and student, working both

ways. Absence of a canon meant interpretation could be inductive, and so rather than being deduced from a seat of authority, the experience of literature was allowed to be a personal affair, albeit shared in a community of others. The teacher's autonomy allowed not only enthusiasm of selection but also a balance of effect. Movement from one text to another need not follow chronology or country. Instead, imaginative interest propelled one through books and authors from any number of eras and cultures, much as an eager reader devours an infinite library. Read individually, these works then became part of that other literary activity, discussion. True, we were not a rich little liberal arts college with class size of a dozen or so, but because there were so many students seeking these courses, scores of filled-up sections could be offered, making enrollments of thirty-five each possible. Thirty-five is no dozen, but it is better than four hundred, as some other departments' lecture classes numbered. In time, I'd come up with various physical strategies to make three dozen seem more like one, but for now it helped just to get out from behind the desk and perch in front of it, projecting myself as in arena theater.

Dr. Hagelman had one more trick to make these lit courses appealing. As an occasional alternate to poetry, fiction, and drama, he persuaded the department to offer specially designed, one-time-only courses filling the same general education requirement but tailored to a specific interest. For the fall of 1972, I drew on my work with Jerzy Kosinski to propose something called "Contemporary Polish-American Literature." Jerzy Kosinski's *Painted Bird* and film scripts by Roman Polanski were at its center, plus heavy doses of currently fashionable Poles in translation (such as Grombrowicz) and an intellectual anchoring in Milosz. Because of the Kosinski-Polanski notoriety, and thanks to the Polish ethnicity of so many NIU students (two-thirds of whom were from Chicago, "the largest Polish city in the world"), it overenrolled into three sections, my full teaching load had I stayed. As it happened, the Kosinski connection had landed me the new job at Northern Iowa, so I left the course to Jim Kennedy, who as the department's resident Marxist would have his hands full with Kosinski's strident anticollectivism and Polanski's refutation of almost every socialist ideal.

The Kosinski connection was beneficial in many ways. While Vonnegut, Sukenick, and Kunen hadn't discouraged my research and were helpful in various ways, Jerzy was so enthusiastic as to dig out anything I wanted himself. Essays, book reviews, privately published pamphlets, even copies

of his two M.A. theses in history and political science from the University of Łodz in Poland—once I'd made contact and begun teaching him, all these things and more came flying through the mails at close intervals. He also put me in touch with another Kosinski scholar, perhaps at that early date the only other one: Dan Cahill at the University of Northern Iowa. Cahill was department head and brought me out for a guest lecture that turned into a job interview and offer. As Northern Illinois was packed solid with bright associate professors and just-promoted fulls, Northern Iowa (where paths to the top were clear) seemed a wiser choice. It was, and not just for the salary and research benefits. What it did for my teaching was an advantage outweighing even the promotion, big raise, and perks.

Although my success with the lecture had assured any skeptics that I wouldn't be a classroom dud, no one expected that I'd thrive in UNI's pedagogical atmosphere. The place was only recently developed from a teachers' college, and my recruitment was considered a first step toward building a publishing faculty. That step was resented, of course, and producing books and articles in such a world made for all the predictable tensions between a lavishly supportive administration and an underpaid (hence validly jealous) older faculty. That wasn't a surprise. What I did find original was the faculty members' approach to curriculum in general and to teaching in particular, especially as they so proudly proclaimed those two things as the full percentage of their duties and essence of their professional lives.

My visiting lecture on a weeknight in June went well enough because I made it lively and comic, making fun of myself and my topic before anyone could lodge serious objections. Yes, I volunteered, *contemporary* was a popular cachet, sure to attract lit students, just as *abnormal* always seemed to draw the crowds in psychology. Here was an idea: why didn't the department try calling its Middle English course "Contemporary Abnormal Chaucer"? They'd have to run multiple sections. This was good, but even better were the examples I'd brought from Vonnegut, Brautigan, and Barthelme, including an audiotape of the president's speech in *Snow White* that had one of my acting students from the *Up* presentation sounding out Barthelme's lines in a perfect Lyndon Johnson voice. I think all thirty department members were there, together with a handful of grad students. Thankfully, it was a cozy room, where I could use arena staging and involve the listeners with my routine, such as having them respond to *Snow White*'s reader questionnaire. With a sense of humor about my work (and in it as well), I seemed safe to be trusted. When my future colleagues heard

that *Innovative Fiction* would be published month after next, not as a scholarly tome or conventional textbook but rather as a "bus-stopper," as one of them put it, the sense of an immediate threat dissolved. By this time next year, the relieved professor assured me, all evidence of the book would have vanished from the earth—after which, he implied, I could get down to the business of being more like him. Why other than for a raise and quick promotion would one do a book anyway? Maybe ten or fifteen years later, when my time came to be considered for full professor, I'd do another, though that certainly wasn't required. This was "a teaching university," he assured me, and my lecture had shown that I could probably teach okay.

Teaching, however, had become politicized. As a reaction against the call to more professional activity, UNI's faculty members had begun claiming that their strength was as teachers—and that nothing whatsoever should detract from it. True, the school had a good reputation for its quality of instruction, but that reputation dated from an older generation and had not been actively renewed. In 1972, an impressive quartet of scholar-teachers was nearing the end of its career: Norman Stageburg, a brilliant linguist with a University of Wisconsin doctorate who had helped found the discipline known as TESOL, the Teaching of English to Speakers of Other Languages; a pair of Yale Ph.D.'s, John Cowley and Louise Forrest, who were importantly *(PMLA!)* if not extensively published on Chaucer and Shakespeare respectively; and the man I'd replaced, Wallace Anderson, author of the most useful book so far on Edwin Arlington Robinson. These four had anchored the English department as the school was transformed from the Iowa State Teachers College to the State College of Iowa and just recently to the University of Northern Iowa. In less than fifteen years, these people had used three different letterheads; no wonder the world wasn't sure just what institution of higher learning was located in Cedar Falls.

What a magnificent state college it must have been back there in the late fifties and through most of the sixties. It gave to the public what elite private schools offered at an immensely higher price: a well-trained, student-oriented faculty with an immense respect for full professional development, all of it taking place on a leafy, hilltop campus at the edge of a lovely riverside town. What survived into the seventies was the memory of this tradition but not its reality. In the middle sixties, when enrollments skyrocketed, the soon-to-be-university's faculty had to be radically expanded just when new doctoral graduates enjoyed the greatest seller's market of all times. Getting one to come out here would have been a miracle;

attracting a dozen and a half was beyond even fantasy. So the administration had taken what was available: a few A.B.D.'s (all-but-dissertations), in most cases A.B.D.'s who'd been let go from their first appointments because they hadn't finished their degrees; high school teachers with enough night and summer classes to earn M.A.'s; and, in more than a few cases, women married to the heads of other departments who'd picked up an M.A. from this same English department as relief from the tedium of volunteer work and social functions.

At UNI, you could be tenured without a Ph.D. But with university status came a concerted administrative push to have everybody get one. Instead of sabbaticals for research, faculty were given PDLs ("Professional Development Leaves") to go back to school and earn a doctorate. Many of these degrees were picked up at the University of Iowa, ninety miles to the south, no one ever questioning the propriety of a tenured faculty member on full pay seeking credentials from a sister institution governed by the same Board of Regents. The English faculty thus recruited enjoyed an unusual benefit of having their doctorates virtually bought for them, with little chance of low grades for course work or examinations being failed. A traveling trophy moved from one member to another as each new doctorate was received. In some cases, these people went from being high school teachers to full professors without ever being a resident doctoral student at all. The notion of a university, so novel here in Cedar Falls, was something the faculty knew very little about.

How all this translated into a curriculum was a disaster. The English major I found at UNI was similar to what I'd seen in its last years at Marquette and already on its way out at Wisconsin. It was the "story of English" sequence evident to some extent at every college and university in America, only here it was being taught with a vengeance. At both undergraduate and graduate levels, period coverage was absolutely mandatory, with no possibilities for even the slightest deviation. The only room for maneuvering was within the Graduate Candidacy Committee, which students had to face early in their first semester of study and declare what courses they'd take for their M.A. If they hadn't taken an Elizabethan literature course as an undergrad, for example, they had to do one now. But would it be in poetry or drama? That depended upon which prof had campaigned his or her way onto the committee, from where one's own particular course could be mandated. What the student preferred or could even argue for logically didn't matter. This was how unpopular or just plain lousy teachers could get their undersubscribed classes filled.

Another prime appointment was to the Graduate Examinations Committee. Here was where the less-than-kindly profs thrived. The exam was an exhaustive one, worse than what I'd faced so miserably for my doctorate—and this was just for an M.A. What appalled me most, though, were the conditions under which it was administered. There was no courtesy or professionalism as at Wisconsin. Instead, the official attitude was one of hostility and suspicion, an adversarial approach that expected students not to display their knowledge and facility but rather to devise ways of cheating. Catching the cheats rather than testing ability seemed to be the committee's goal.

Both the nature of the questions and the manner of their asking were groomed accordingly. Talk about cheating—the exam committee delighted in trick questions, creating impossible conundrums sure to lead even the best student into making mistakes. This testing method snagged far more of the brighter candidates, whose solid preparation made them ripe for such intricacies, than dull ones, who never rose to the bait. Points were docked if someone failed to hyphenate *Moby-Dick* or added an apostrophe to *Finnegans Wake.* Interpretation was limited to regurgitation of what had been taught in class, with sometimes disastrous results: if in 1972 a student discussed Wordsworth not in the manner of Cleanth Brooks but of Geoffrey Hartman (a name the examiners would not recognize and a methodology they would disallow), that meant failure, too. All this trickery and incompetence was administered in a small, locked room. Fire regulations be damned—this was an *examination,* confound it! If students could not endure a four-hour session without a bathroom break, they were told by one graduate director to bring a can or wear what railroad and subway personnel called a "motorman's friend."

A quarter century later, one of our new recruits—the first since me to arrive with both doctorate and book publications in hand—tried to change this. His question was a simple one. How did we test our own abilities when writing a critical essay: by setting aside a few weeks, collecting the books we needed for reference, drafting some ideas, and eventually coming up with a decent piece of work, or by locking ourselves in a closet for half a day with nothing but bluebooks and a pen? Although by this time the faculty had begun to change, there were still enough of the old crowd around that the idea was for a time hooted down.

My view of this faculty is harsh and perhaps even more harshly expressed. But I have a specifically pedagogical reason. It was indeed a weak group of individuals, as they themselves admitted; during one memorable

university faculty meeting, their spokesperson, David Crownfield from philosophy and religion (which had been part of the English department a few years before when he'd been hired), scolded the provost that unreasonable demands were being made, that he and his cohort from the midsixties hirings were "the best you could get at the time, and now you're stuck with us." But weak as they were, these people were much closer to the national average than were the distinguished faculties at Stanford and Berkeley or Harvard and Yale. That's where the leaders were in both teaching methods and curricular development, let alone scholarship. The point is that my colleagues in Cedar Falls were not about to follow these innovators, nor do I expect were most other average and less-than-average faculties. It's a sad truth that so many English departments muck along at their own levels of minimal competence, incapable of building a sound logic for their existence because nobody takes them seriously. They don't even take themselves seriously. What does matter to them is politics—local to be sure, and petty at the best. And the prime political concern for anyone is personal territory: steal my purse and you steal trash, but take away my Elizabethan Nondramatic Prose class and you're in for the fight of your life.

All this made it clear to me that reforming the teaching of literature had to happen elsewhere. Administrative attempts to shape up the English department just made things worse, as presidents, provosts, deans, and a series of beleaguered heads only served to focus animosities. If there was anything worse than the committee dealing with student requirements, it was the group deciding faculty retention: the Tenure Board, or in its contractually formalized version, the Professional Assessment Committee, called "PAC," as in "wolfpack." Just as the graduate faculty was not much of a faculty per se, for anyone with a Ph.D. was customarily admitted whether or not he or she had the intention of pursuing scholarship, PAC consisted of everybody in the department who was tenured. Two members would visit each candidates's classes (twice each) and study the files, but discussion and evaluation were wide open, and all members voted equally, whether informed or not. Therefore, a couple minutes of perfunctory analysis was followed by an hours-long hen session in which the person being considered was pecked apart. Sadly, professional achievement was a tertiary consideration to whether the candidate was liked by the administration and considered a threat to the status quo.

Worst of all were the cases where consideration never even took place. One year, before the PAC process could begin, someone noticed that a candidate's personnel file had some administrative technicalities mixed

up—nothing serious, just a matter of misdotted i's and uncrossed t's. Look at this, the person claimed: here was a once-in-a-lifetime chance to embarrass the provost, whose error it was. Great idea, the others agreed, throwing the case out, even though the candidate was widely liked, exceptionally qualified, and obviously deserving of tenure.

How could they do this, I railed. What had the candidate done to deserve this? The problem was with administrative paperwork he'd been unable to see! Well, came their answer, the refusal to consider his case had nothing to do with him at all. His tenure was not the issue; what mattered was that the university had erred, and here was the opportunity to exercise faculty power and make fools of the people over in Gilchrist Hall. Principles were more important than individuals, power more important than good judgment. It certainly wasn't anything *personal.*

Literature draws on the utmost sensitivity to deal with the deepest parts of the human soul. How could these people be even halfway decent stewards of poetry, fiction, and drama when they so easily consigned actual living human beings to ruin just so they could gain such fleeting annoyance of an administrator, and not even an evil administrator at that, just a bright young woman to whom most of our faculty objected because of her rank, gender, and age? And the guy being sacrificed was supposedly their friend!

I often wondered how I myself had won tenure, only to remember how it happened by means of a political backfire. When I'd been recruited in 1972, tenure still came after three years, a remnant of the sixties' mad rush to build a university when new faculty were in short supply. By my second year in Cedar Falls, I had three books out, a fourth accepted for publication, good class visits, and astronomically high student evaluations. Thinking I'd jump to a better job elsewhere, the department head, dean, and provost all wanted to give me early tenure—not necessarily as a reward, but most certainly to restrict my mobility. I took it the first way and was thrilled, but my tenured colleagues urged me to turn it down. Let the recommendation come from them next year, and faculty power would remain intact. It would be automatic, they assured me. One of the more emotional profs pledged to resign in protest if my case were in any way hindered. So I agreed, only to have it blocked next year. As it happened, a candidate one step behind me was put up by the administration for similar early tenure, and to her credit, she refused to cave in to PAC. There was nothing the faculty could say to this nomination of such a qualified person without violating the principles of Affirmative Action, so they held my case in abeyance until the administration backed down on her. Do wolf-

packs hold hostages? Maybe hyenas do. Such creatures do not make good stewards of literature.

No decent literature curriculum could ever hope to evolve in this squalid world of petty politics, politics that flourished in a climate of self-defeatism. And here is another reason not to hope for such reform from the Harvards and Yales of this world. Like the impossible hourglass figures and rippling muscles held out as physical ideals to American women and men, respectively, Ivy League and Stanford-Berkeley faculties boast professional profiles well beyond the abilities of English teachers at Moo U to achieve. Any attempt at mimicry only leads to worse disappointment. What succeeds at Berkeley or Brown is almost sure to breed dissatisfaction at a place like Northern Iowa, named not for an attractive location or prestigious founder or even for a state or city but rather for a nebulous, amorphous region reminiscent of the old radio comedy moniker of *Southwestern North Dakota State University at Hoople.*

Not that people wherever they are don't deserve a higher education— only that one has to be honest about the availability of faculty. The students, more often than you'd think, can be as good as at Harvard—at least none are here because of ancestry, connections, or money. And new faculty, especially when recruited from integral programs with their degrees obtained the honest way, can do wonders when allowed to work with these undergraduates. But in such circumstances, deadwood can obstruct healthy growth and change for up to half a century, so deeply do the older faculty's disappointments run.

It is sad to see how disappointments as well as anxieties can become institutionalized. In 1976, four years after I'd joined it, the UNI faculty voted for collective bargaining. The union itself campaigned for this vote in outright anti-intellectual fashion, promising to fight for fewer research benefits and more teaching duties, all of it rewarded with across-the-board raises. The only advantages went to the very old staffers who'd been held back for decades by their M.A. degrees and lack of professional activity. These folks now got massive pay boosts for time in grade. The administration won out on preserving merit portions (about 30 percent) in any raises bargained, which meant people like me got both, pushing our salaries disproportionately higher thanks to a percentage base shared with the lowest earners. Every year, the union would solemnly provide a budget-book analysis of each salary line to its members, just the depressing news it could only be confounding to see.

With so many of UNI's assets squandered on extraneous matters (bargaining alone cost millions), faculty salaries fell even further behind those at the University of Iowa and at Iowa State, where the Regents gave those schools whatever UNI had gained plus a full 100 percent of merit money for raises. This, in turn, made some of my colleagues feel justified to teach their eight and nine o'clock classes and then leave for a full day's and evening's employment in the private sector, doing everything from selling computers at Target to becoming a grandly successful car salesman. One prof ran a retail business and held office hours there; another was notorious for keeping student advisees with appointments waiting in the hall while he brokered real estate. Yet all of this was excused because these folks never "stole time from their students" to engage in research and publication, which the union branded as scabbing. Yet for all the cars sold and condominiums leased, there was no professional satisfaction, just a chip-on-the-shoulder attitude toward the whole university scene. It was not a pretty picture, and I never saw anyone very happy in it.

Self-defeatism extended to curricula as well. The courses I taught were advanced but remained reasonably accessible to general readers. There was the American Renaissance with a bow to Emerson and Thoreau, close attention to Hawthorne and Melville, and time left for some of Poe's wilder fiction, including *The Narrative of Arthur Gordon Pym*. Realism and Naturalism stressed Twain's vernacular language and the interface between Howells's manners and Norris's muscular aesthetics; Crane and James I handled in less extent as inbred, hothouse products. My favorite course was the Twentieth-Century American Novel, which I taught as in DeKalb: one-third moderns (Hemingway-Fitzgerald-Faulkner), one-third contemporary (Updike-Bellow-Malamud), and one-third "postcontemporary," the term I'd begun using for an ever-changing group of new writers I guessed would be a good bet for the future.

All three, but especially the twentieth-century one, began attracting nonmajors. There were history, philosophy, art, music, and modern language students to be sure, but also plenty of business majors who either wanted to get some polish or just use up an elective to escape (for three wonderful hours a week) the tedious pressure of their accounting or marketing courses. Thus, instead of the customary ten or twelve students, I had twenty-five, the enrollment limit, and could have had more. Soon, the novel course was running two sections, the only advanced class to do so.

Wouldn't Charles Hagelman be proud? Look at the credit hours I was

generating: over five hundred per year, and all in advanced courses that would otherwise top out at a hundred at best. The mass sections of Humanities I and II, taught like a high school honors course, were doing better, thanks to class sizes appropriate to the huge lecture halls where instruction took place. Indeed, I began thinking of my own course as an alternative or even antidote to the reductive humanities program. Given everything that came up in this century's novels, one could not help but cover the essentials of Western culture, especially when students with such diverse preparation could contribute to the discussion.

At this point, the department's Curriculum Committee intervened. Nonmajors flocking to an advanced course? This could not be allowed to happen. Think of how the purity of our majors' education would be diluted, not to mention how they'd be sullied by such contact with the unclean followers of other, less pure disciplines. Committee members did not go so far as restricting my course to majors only, though they may have wanted to—university regulations prevented that. But the committee was able to post a long string of prerequisites, the same as for becoming an English major, so the job was done. My classes still filled, but with students of our own kind, which made things a little dull. My colleagues' courses, however, got thinner, until enrollments in some became so low that a two-year rotational plan had to be implemented lest too many classes not "make" and be dropped. What a waste, but at least our department could say it was more interested in "standards" than in money—and besides, money was something for the department head to worry about. I myself would have argued that the loss was to curricular health, invigorated as it had been for a while by all that new student blood. But nobody wanted to hear any of that!

A year later, when I was away from meetings for my first sabbatical, this same Curriculum Committee looked over the three top-drawing graduate seminars: Contemporary Fiction, Contemporary Poetry, and Contemporary Drama. For whatever reason, it decided to meld them into one: Contemporary Literature. Needless to say, seminar enrollments plummeted, and three properly focused entities were corrupted into a single course, which had to contract itself by becoming a survey.

How can a faculty be so self-destructive? Well, it was the midseventies, hardly a brilliant era of achievement. The war was going badly, the economy ready to fall apart, the profession enduring its toughest times in two generations, and everything seeming to promise only worse. About this time,

the initial contract-mandated review took place. For the first time ever, old timers had to have student evaluations. This group, of course, had cultivated the reputation of being brilliant teachers; after all, that was why they didn't let distractions like reading and writing intervene. Now, students were asked if they agreed. Sadly, the two most revered "great teachers" failed miserably. One, it turned out, was mentally debilitated, though you couldn't tell it from his manner—only tasks that had to be organized, like class meetings, were for him chaotic. Another had been spending entire semesters never getting beyond the first few pages of the first assigned reading; that material would be repeated for the initial ten minutes of each class, after which a monologue would ensue about a long-estranged spouse and deeply loved family pets. Each, miraculously, continued, though with the word so embarrassingly out the two became teachers to be avoided. At least they weren't working other jobs; you can't sell Subarus when suffering from Alzheimer's or dementia.

On paper, the department looked even worse. For the review, everyone was asked to prepare a curriculum vitae. By this time, I had six books, a couple dozen essays, a few MLA convention papers, and a string of lectures given coast to coast, so mine looked fine. For others, the results were odd. Several filled pages naming every department committee they'd served on, one of them enumerating motions made. Another poor soul listed the magazines to which she subscribed, a supposed-to-be-smart list including *Harper's,* the *New Yorker,* and the *Saturday Review.* Three outside evaluators were to visit and write reports, but the head, ever fearful of mutiny, let the faculty choose their own. A trio of old mentors did the job, telling the regents how their former students and the rest of us were the best things since sliced bread and canned beer. Only two decades later, when a tougher head brought in some truly unbiased experts, did the truth come out.

For too many years, such was the style: faculty cared little beyond their own turfs (and those off-campus jobs), while saving potentially creative energies for politics. Department heads were democratically chosen but rarely allowed to serve out their terms—no matter how popular the start, dissension would always bring them down. As the job market had tightened, qualified young faculty would be recruited only to be driven away by the hideous atmosphere. Except for good friends in other departments and in the community, I would have been pretty lonesome, for people like me didn't last in English hereabouts. Fresh arrivals, who in this new market had doctorates, experience, and publications, were treated like prac-

tice teachers, presumed to be inept and incomplete until they learned from the masters. From time to time, I'd come across statements by sometime English profs such as Mark Harris and Dick Higgins, who from outside the ivory tower would wonder how people with the loveliest job on earth, conveying the treasure of literary art to bright young adults, could behave like such disagreeable monsters or at the very least seem less like professors of literature than professors of government. A new UNI president, who did much to reform things, ventured in dismay that while he himself was "goal oriented," the English faculty here seemed "procedures oriented." One of my colleagues responded by writing a letter to the student newspaper equating the new leader with Hitler and Mussolini. Another colleague, when facing the new requirement of filing an annual service report, complained in a department meeting that this was like "being given a one-way ticket to Auschwitz." He wasn't Jewish.

Not every English department in America had moments like these, but I'll bet many have. Only a few are remarkably better, and these constitute the far extremes: either superstar faculties at the top universities, where an era's innovations were introduced (deconstruction at Yale, multicultural studies at Berkeley, semiotics at Brown) or the teaching staff at Bible colleges, where integrity of faith keeps people on track. Between these was the great middle: universities where the English department would be every provost's worst headache, for most of the same reasons evident here at UNI.

I wish that I could prove how such deep-seated and widespread unhappiness among English faculties was due to problems with the literature curriculum. But that would involve using the tools of psychology, sociology, and human resource management, well beyond the competence of a personal memoir. Suffice it to say that even if in its ideal form the old English major could be taught successfully, the reality of what UNI's and so many other universities' departments were confirms how hopeless practical conditions had become. It just wasn't working here, and far too many other English faculties around the country were in similar if less histrionic conditions.

If you're not part of the solution, you're part of the problem. This folk wisdom from the radical sixties summed up my position in a novel way, for I was part of both. Had I and others like me not been recruited, or had I and these few others given up and left (as many in fact did), UNI's English department could have plodded on into the twenty-first century with its ideals from the nineteenth century intact. Volkswagen sales and con-

dominium lease-ups would have soared. But here I was, proving that you didn't have to work a second full-time job to earn a living, and your classes needn't go to hell if you took time to read books and write about them. This didn't win me very many friends in the department, so in terms of morale, I was certainly part of the problem. As far as the solution, I tried working inside the system long and hard, pleading for reform, and in time it came. But for emotional survival, it was necessary to find solace elsewhere. And so I drifted away from the department, avoiding especially the types of meetings that would make me angry. Everyone had heard my outrage enough, and in terms of democratic procedures, one vote (or the two or three my oratory might sometimes gather) was not going to change anything.

However, the university administration (from department on up through dean and provost to the regents themselves) was fabulously supportive, as had been NIU's back in DeKalb. There, my chance discovery of novelist Willard Motley's papers had led to a meeting with the president himself, fresh from his previous job as CEO of Inland Steel—that's what a mess of the upper administration Kent State had made. He authorized the acquisition-on-loan of Motley's archives, and soon I had a crew of students and interested colleagues digging through the genesis of *Knock on Any Door* and the author's other work, most of us publishing essays on our finds. Here at UNI the president intervened to have our library buy a massive but unique collection of works by the key American fiction writers to emerge in the sixties—not just jacketed first editions of their novels and story collections but everything else they'd published, too, including small-press poetry volumes and textbooks that never made it onto libraries' shelves. It was a treasure trove, making our library the best resource for this subject in the country, and even more so than with the Motley papers, I knew graduate work could flourish with such materials. But when my department colleagues responded by changing requirements to make such work virtually impossible, I didn't even bother to object—by this time, who could care?

To keep happy, I let my interests drift elsewhere. Friendships came easy among profs and staffers in other departments, especially history, art, philosophy, French, German, and music, where there were no morale problems as in English. By the eighties, I was publishing books in these fields. For a while, I taught a special course called "The American 1960s," which treated Richard Nixon and John F. Kennedy as fiction writers, Ken Kesey

and Joseph Heller as politicians, Frank O'Hara and Bob Dylan as public spokespersons, and so forth. Our campus boasted two excellent FM radio stations, one of which covered the upper Midwest with 100,000 watts of power blasting out blues and progressive rock twenty-four hours a day, and some of our course sessions were held in the studio. Once again, my class was full of nonmajors. Discussion among this diverse group was excellent, and soon I published a book from it, *The American 1960s: Imaginative Acts in a Decade of Change.* Its subtitle expressed the method our class had used, studying not an aesthetic canon but rather a process, a broadly cultural activity. Once again, it was as Ron Sukenick would put it, "not *art* but *act.*"

During the sixties, I'd played in bands, first to earn spending money in high school and then to pay Marquette University's expensive tuition. The best of them, the only really professional outfit, had taken me on during my senior year, when to sock away some money for marriage and grad school, I was desperate enough to work six nights a week. Junior and the Classics was a black rhythm-and-blues band that could get booked into white clubs only by having a couple of white members, a role I filled on baritone sax. That's how I had learned about imaginative acts in music for that hyperactive decade, seeing it happen from the inside as pop music took on African American characteristics with an exuberance unmatched in music history. Now, just ten years later, I could teach what I had learned— plus have the chance to reexperience the music again. The opportunity came from a friend in broadcasting, Bob Dorr, who after helping pioneer the campus FM stations as a student intern, graduated to become their music director. He produced and hosted his own rock and blues history shows and, as the drummer in a rock band similar to the one I had in high school, was eager to launch a new one synthesizing all that he'd learned since. I was the only lit prof he knew, as most other departments in the humanities tended to regard the English faculty as (in the words of art professor Roy Behrens, with whom I'd do a book) "a bunch of tight-assed critics." But when I played Bob the old 45 single of Junior's "Wise Up," he judged me loose enough to help him form a band.

This had to be for fun, I emphasized, not wanting to be like the car salesmen and realtors whose full-time jobs made mockery of their faculty positions. Not to worry, he assured me: he doubted any jobs could be booked for a year and then just the occasional Saturday night gig. Surely I deserved a hobby, he argued, adding that he'd never worked as a pro and would appreciate some good counsel. Call it a teaching experience, he

urged. So as I taught my course on the American sixties and Bob broad-cast "Progression" and "Only Blues," our group began practicing.

We called the band "Raggs," for its raggedy membership of castoffs. Bob soon abandoned the drums to come up front with vocals and harmonica. I played tenor sax; with a student on electric piano and organ, a drop-out on guitar, an unemployed country and western musician on bass, and a Vietnam vet rehabbing at the local V.A. hospital on drums, we made a tight, six-piece group.

The band did great. It only took us five months to get into shape, and by summer we were booked as often as four nights weekly. Though I knew I'd have to quit when school resumed in the fall, I could enjoy it now as a lab for my sixties research. Like so much of that decade's culture, we in-verted familiar expectations to make things fresh and interesting—*defa-miliarizing* the experience, as theorists would say, doing it all in the step-by-step process used in my *Innovative Fiction* anthology and teaching. Like both of these classroom projects, we could feel the thrill of participatory performance when everything goes well.

I worried that all this might look like moonlighting, but the university took it the other way. My weekends were my own, and I was in fact using them as research experience for both my course and my writing. Both lo-cal dailies plus the student newspaper did stories on my work, and one night I looked down from the bandstand to see two sets of people on the floor: on one side, the university president, provost, and graduate dean with their spouses, on the other, the faculty union's president and chief nego-tiator. Other than in bargaining sessions, these two groups never met—labor law may well have forbidden it. But here they were, dancing to my music, with me calling the tune.

As classes resumed that fall, and I left the band, I noticed something: while the music business had invigorated my teaching, critical writing lagged behind—there was only so much energy to expend. To compen-sate, I developed a new way of presenting my research, something more akin to the way I taught literature: in spatially juxtaposed page designs, using collages and different typefaces that removed any need for connec-tive tissue, the stuff I'd always thought was dull blather in print and re-dundancies in class. Why not let the materials speak for themselves in tell-ing arrangements that the eye could appraise at a glance? With Roy Behrens from the art department, I put together one such essay on Donald Bar-thelme for *Critique,* drawing a happy response from him that started off

our friendship. A dozen others followed in a spin-off from the band's energy that year, appearing in *Chicago Review, TriQuarterly,* and other journals, until they added up to a book. It all seemed a graphic equivalent of what I was doing with my life, so as *The Life of Fiction,* it was dedicated first to my children and second to band leader Bob Dorr and another musician with whom I'd become friends, Michael Johnson, who prefaced the book as personally as Jim Kunen had done for *Innovative Fiction:*

> I could sing you a song about the happier days
> But the happier days ain't here—
> String you along in a million ways
> And only the lies would be clear.
> You need something to believe in, right or wrong—,
> You'd sell your soul tomorrow for a song.

Did I make such a sale? It was indeed a time of great transition for me, and one of the changes was shared with my wife. We'd had what was commonly described as an open marriage. For a time, the quasi-communal nature of the band was a natural development of our extended family style, but as Raggs reformed at the end of the year, so did we, each taking a new partner for keeps. Talk about a life of fiction: Elaine and I were reinventing ourselves, settling on firmer identities after a decade of almost constant change. She headed off to law school in Iowa City and an eventual career in Chicago. The kids and I stayed in Cedar Falls, where life settled down in more traditional patterns—but never unquestioned traditions, for in taking family trips to enjoy scenic pleasures Elaine had never thought appealing, we could savor as special what others took for granted. In similar manner, I took the kids out to discover minor-league baseball, a whole other world that seemed (and was) as complex, involved, and self-contained as the band life they'd been witnessing. Even the band profited. With a new (and much better) horn man, they renamed themselves the Blue Band and got good enough that Dorr would quit his job with the campus radio station and devote himself full time to bookings and promotions. Maybe I could have stayed with them. But my son was eager to start learning on my tenor sax, so I turned it over to him. From sax, he went on to guitar, becoming a far better musician than I ever was (and, thanks to his job as a newspaperman, more widely published as well). Children do seem to pick their parents' avocations for their own more successful vocations. Today, Jonathan leads Iowa City's best blues band, giving Dorr his only real state-

wide competition. There were still new things I wanted to do in the class-room and other books to write, so as the seventies closed, I seized the chance to move beyond the sixties class, which without the band as a stimulus might well have gone stale.

Fiction as invention: this awareness had emerged from my work with the band and with the innovative writers I was teaching. Given how fiction derives from life but also provides models for living, wasn't it obvious that personally pertinent invention was at the heart of it? As my first wife and I each remarried, we were undertaking such invention ourselves, she becoming a lawyer and the careerist she'd always wanted to be, me settling into the role of paterfamilias. My new wife had interests and training so different from my own, including a just-completed B.A. in anthropology and an M.A. underway in Spanish (to complement her mastery of French), that the world we shared seemed new. She was also an Iowa native and could show me and her new stepchildren a secret beauty my first wife and I, still oriented to Milwaukee and Chicago, never knew existed. Talk about reinvention and the life of fiction: in no time flat Elaine was in a high-rise apartment overlooking Lakeshore Drive in her beloved Second City, while Julie and I were roasting marshmallows with the kids in Yellow River Forest and climbing limestone ridges among Indian mounds high above the Mississippi. All turned out well. As I write two decades later, we're looking forward to Sunday's christening of our first grandchild, where the whole extended family will be gathering. So there's evidence that this part of the theory works.

The band may well have helped push us all toward the final step, which was good, but keeping up with its growing professionalism was too much work to continue. Consequently, after I left it, a renewed interest had room to develop, within both my nuclear family and my teaching. The activity was an old love, baseball, reborn now as I gave Julie some precious free time by taking the kids out to the ballpark. A minor-league contest, it was my first game in over a dozen years—half my adult lifetime, in fact, since the Braves had left Milwaukee and broken my heart. Now, deep affections came alive once more. For Jonathan and Nina, it was love at first sight. For the next ten years ('til they left for college), we were out there for almost every home game and a few road games in Wisconsin and Illinois as well. I tell the story in *Owning a Piece of the Minors,* for that's just what happened: one night buying three tickets, and within a year helping run the operation. It was a nonprofit civic volunteer group that did the work, so my par-

ticipation earned me points with the university for community service. But more important were the recreational and eventual professional benefits for me and the kids alike. As single-digit midgets, Jonathan started sportswriting on baseball for the local shopper paper, while Nina organized several businesses around the operation, including can redemption and popcorn vending. While still being Dad each evening, I picked up new ideas for my books and for the classroom, so everyone came out ahead.

Before, I'd shaped both my research and my classroom work according to innovations in fiction. The only problem was that professionally and pedagogically innovative fiction was considered elitist and inaccessible. I'd fought those labels on paper and in person, showing how practical these literary experiments could be. Yet even with Kurt Vonnegut as a great example of how such radically fictive art can be anchored in solidly middle-class and traditionally American values, students and general readers could still be daunted by their first view of something like *Slaughterhouse-Five*. But consider how appealing would be a piece of baseball fiction. That the subgenre had such a lowbrow reputation made it all the easier to allay fears that anything woolly and abstruse was going on. After all, baseball was as common and unthreatening as could be. Baseball's initially *declassé* image also kept it safe from the hectoring interference of the English curriculum. Among university types, football was still king—not our own college team, God help them, but NFL football of the Sunday afternoon and Monday night variety. These were the only times you could find my department colleagues paying attention to athletics. For baseball fans at UNI, I had to look to other departments. Hal Wohl from history liked to come out with me and the kids, for example, to relive his Ebbets Field childhood. German professor Jim Knowlton (with whom I was writing a book on Peter Handke) loved the junk food and amused himself with the inane chatter of the baseball wives and groupies sitting just behind us. Art professor Frje Echeverria stretched a canvas and from our seats painted one huge acrylic, then another, of the field and stands as evening turned to night and the stadium lights took effect. When young Americanist scholars from abroad came to visit me and use the university library's sixties fiction collection, I'd bring them to a game, often with hilarious results. About this time, the English department hired a bright new specialist in children's and young adult reading, Jeff Copeland, who because he was such a lively teacher and aggressive researcher, at once suffered hounding by the worst elements of our faculty. To get away from it, he came out to the ballpark, where the

two of us became close friends. He too wound up becoming a director, but of more consequence he is now, fifteen years later, the head of an almost totally reformed English department, where none of the harassment he and I suffered could happen today.

The benefits of all this to my teaching were substantial and extensive. At base, it settled my personal life into a nourishing pattern that made everything easier and "funner" (the kids' term) to do. Having baseball come around with the seasons gave things a more cyclic (and hence more sensible) feeling, and I'd resume fall teaching refreshed and remade. During the winter, our monthly board meetings kept me in touch with the real world of nuts and bolts, dollars and cents. Yes, we were a nonprofit operation, and none of us took a penny for his or her efforts, but we had to be careful not to go bankrupt. Over the year, a million dollars would come in and go out—end up a little to the good, and we could buy a new tarp, go the other way, and the Cleveland Indians would have to lend us money until the cash flow resumed with preseason ticket and advertising sales. Business was handled by our single full-time employee, a graduate-trained general manager. Having the kids involved made it a family thing, but not in the clichéd manner of "quality time" that gets so many parents and their offspring either bored silly by static focus or overactivitied to death. The games were a real and regular part of our lives, something we did together for both fun and purpose. We didn't just sit there, though there was plenty of time for that, especially when Julie came along, and the kids and I could show off our new toy. Among our regular seatmates, an extended family developed, and one of the more obvious benefits was the chance I got to talk with someone besides professors—a good technique to master before trying to have genuine discussion in class. Most surprising and of greatest professional importance was that becoming part of this baseball operation let me see that you didn't have to be an avant-gardist to free fiction from the restraint of misunderstood conventions. As I should have known from Kurt Vonnegut's work, you could find all you needed in the commonest American culture right before you, which in my case now was baseball. Here was something that in theory could hold its own with Roland Barthes and Jacques Derrida but which was as familiar as the nicest childhood memories and adult rediscoveries.

The key was recognizing something any sandlot player or weekend softballer knows: baseball provides a perfect fiction, while not demanding the suspension of disbelief. Players and fans wouldn't use these terms,

of course, but in practice, both the game as played and as observed is as constructively self-evident as any Vonnegut novel or story by Grace Paley.

Think about it: like even the most traditional narrative, baseball has characters, a plot, action, development, crisis, and resolution. All these narrative factors can be enhanced by imagery, allegory, symbolism, and the like. The only difference, and what makes it like the innovations of someone so radical as Ronald Sukenick, is that you don't have to pretend that they are real. Let's start with the characters. All are quite practical identities, yet with obviously invented qualities and roles to play. The first baseman, for example, will be tall (for a good reach when covering the line or holding a runner on base) and will often be left-handed (for the same two reasons). The shortstop, however, is nimble and quick—and never left-handed, or double-play throws to the second baseman would be undoable. All other positions have their same unique logic, even down to the relatively new roles of designated hitter (old and slow but with a powerful swing) and closer (a madman). The action these characters advance is similarly artificial but compelling, a progression of balls and strikes, hits and errors, runs and outs through nine innings of opposition—until at the end one team wins. Like the twelve-bar blues format I'd loved so much with the band, baseball's structure is reductively simple yet infinitely expansive, all done with the audience's full awareness of how made-up it is, yet deeply interesting and often exciting.

It took just a couple years to get enough feel for the operation to start writing baseball, a phrase I used to mimic the "Talkin' Baseball" song then popular. One did not write *about* baseball—you wrote baseball itself, with no need for distance from the subject because the game, like innovative fiction, did not represent anything beyond its own action. To be sure, there were those who tried to write about it in a way that made it symbolic of everything from the American way of life to nature's grand renewal. But for me, that approach meant reams of turgid prose and circuses of preening poses, neither of which I wanted for my own work either on the page or in the classroom. I did not want to become "Professor Baseball," even though there were talented academics who cashed in on such labels. This was not ofay intellectual slumming for me, and at the park I kept my university affiliation to myself, acting and dressing more like a roofer on break than the Cambridge don folks thought they were getting, just as at school I disappointed some folks by not coming to class in spikes and jersey. This was the end of the seventies and start of the eighties, remember, when you'd

find certain profs dressing in singlet and hose to teach Shakespeare's history plays, which made as much sense to me as getting oneself up as a corncob to teach Faulkner's *Sanctuary*. I wanted my baseball work to come quietly, easily, and naturally, and thankfully that's how it happened.

Most of all, I just loved being at the ballpark and started writing to prolong the experience, at least imaginatively. I soon had enough short stories growing from the experience to start submitting, with occasional success. They eventually came together as a cycle, *Short Season,* which followed a fictive team through the April-to-end-of-August schedule common to all minor-league teams. I taught the book because students asked me to, as happened later with the sequel to it, *Basepaths,* and *Writing Baseball,* an anthology the University of Illinois Press asked me to assemble. All this work caught the eye of Richard Peterson, the former English department head at Southern Illinois University, who was celebrating his relief from administrative work by diving into the teaching and criticism of baseball literature. He took interest in my fiction and invited me to join his SIU Press project of establishing a curricular resource—easy enough, especially as Pete wanted to call it the "Writing Baseball" series. By this time, I was writing books on philosophy, art, jazz, and air force historiography and working those disciplines into my lit class, so I probably wasn't as focused on baseball as some folks wished.

In the meantime, baseball had provided an unusual but effective bridge to interests abroad. My remarriage prompted the start of frequent trans-Atlantic travels, returning from Paris just in time for opening day and then leaving for Ireland right after the season's close on August 31. On one of these final nights, our pitcher tossed me the game ball, I stuck it in my coat pocket and a day and a half later placed it on the grave of William Butler Yeats at Drumcliff in County Mayo. With the luck of the Irish, my academic year had been reformed. By taking myself out of the running for a distinguished professorship elsewhere, UNI had rewarded me with a six-hour teaching schedule (as opposed to the conventional nine-hour load), and so that I wouldn't miss any classes, the administration decided it would be best if I taught my two courses in a concentrated half-semester format. Hence, I taught doubletime for the second half of first semester (generally October 21 to December 8) and the first half of the second (usually running January 14 or so through the end of February). Thus, April in Paris followed by a summer of baseball climaxing with a September and early October on Dartmoor and in Connemara was a practical schedule. There

was nothing privileged to it; these half-semester courses were available to any faculty who wished to teach them and were widely demanded by the students, and by staying in one-star hotels in France and B-and-Bs in Britain and Ireland, Julie and I could make do on less than twenty dollars a day (granted, meals were out of backpacks, and airline tickets were bought half a year ahead at deep discounts). My mother alternated with Julie's sisters as live-in nurture for the children, so it all worked out well. Anybody with even a working-class salary could have done it, and in time, my mother, the kids, and Julie's family would come along.

The other change in duties was accidental. One half-semester early on, my department head at the time asked if I could help out by doing the unthinkable and teach two sections of the widely scorned general education course Introduction to Literature. I'd taught something like it before at DeKalb, of course, and loved it, so why not here? In the new intensive format, it went so well that I astonished the department by refusing to give it up, saying goodbye to graduate seminars and advanced majors courses forever. What I taught best, it turned out, didn't fit within the existing program—I had to go out of the department and into gen ed to find happiness. Could it be possible that an English education made one resistant to the literature of one's time?

My course's success delighted the administration and annoyed the English department faculty. Attempts were made to rescind the instructor autonomy that made my experiments possible and impose a unified booklist and syllabus, something that failed only because other departments in the college were offering their own versions and needed to insure independence. In one department meeting, an older prof spoke up nostalgically for his student days, when everyone was reading the same books and could thus have "rap sessions" (yes) out of class. I responded by saying students should be getting on with their own lives out of class, then threw gasoline on the fire by citing John Cage's dismay at his first college lit class, where thirty students were all reading the same book instead of thirty different ones and comparing their experiences. Later on, when I discovered how working with literature helped students improve their own writing, another hostile instructor challenged me to show results. At my own expense, I photocopied seventy papers from my two sections and turned them over, at which point he claimed they were all plagiarized (though there were no library sources on these brand new writers) or copied from dorm and frat house files (though I did different books each semester) or written by ex-

perts (though I was the only expert on these particular figures). He finally admitted he was being a poor loser but didn't want to know how my students had succeeded.

But enough of this department nonsense. It wasn't the department from hell—from purgatory, perhaps, and because it was like so many others across the United States, my frustration bears study. By 1980, I'd served my time and won entry into heaven, which teaching Intro to Lit has become. Here's how.

3
Teaching

Since 1980, I've taught almost nothing but the general education class Introduction to Literature, two sections each semester. The rare exceptions, which can be counted on the fingers of one hand, just prove the rule it had taken me fourteen years of previous teaching to learn: I really don't like working at any level of the standard English curriculum, nor is literature very well taught there.

I only got the course because nobody else wanted it. Taking it over made me look good, an enhancement to the University of Northern Iowa's reputation that at our school teaching comes first. Having a widely published scholar made accessible to gen ed students was a rather surprising way of keeping this promise, so there were rewards (reaching all the way to special recognition at a formal dinner with the State Board of Regents). But the best were in the classroom, where I now felt closest to the process of literature. It didn't happen when writing fiction myself—that was too solitary. Nor did it occur when I'd get involved with writers like Kurt Vonnegut and Jerzy Kosinski and their ongoing concerns—that was important fun, too, but ultimately more of a business nature. For me, literature came alive in the course meetings, where both my own writing and my association with more prominent writers could be made useful by helping students figure out how to deal with such books.

Sure, some might say, it's just a captive audience for one's indulgences. But that could only happen in a graduate seminar, and probably only in a graduate seminar at Berkeley or Yale. This was the University of Northern Iowa, with general education students who didn't know me or my authors and who couldn't care less. Yet before any offering of this course was a third of the way done, they did care about the literature—because it was making sense to them in a way too many traditionally taught classes

prevented. The success, which I measured not just by discussion and pa-pers but by class evaluations each semester, was due to both subject mat-ter and method, each of which was unique.

The structure was special to begin with, and as happens in the world of good design, the proper mechanics followed. Half-semester scheduling certainly accommodated my research travels, but I stick with it mainly because pedagogically it worked so well—not even the crassest of profes-sors could enjoy April in Paris and September on Dartmoor when his or her classes were bad. It turned out that students loved what they called "intensive" courses. Rather than dragging things out, these half-semester courses with their double-length meeting times got right to the important stuff and then stopped before getting boring. The set-up had stayed in place anachronistically, a remnant of the old days when education students did their practice teaching over half a semester and needed an array of short courses for the rest. They remained as "alternate delivery systems," an edu-cationist phrase that conferred a blessing to my experimental doings. Re-cruiters in the Admissions Office could show how we were bending over backwards to serve students. The Scheduling Office found double peri-ods a nuisance, but I solved that problem by picking dead hours such as noontime and late afternoon. Using teacherly tricks, I maintained almost perfect attendance, even late on Fridays, when the campus was deserted. Students simply wanted classes this way, and they were willing to take extra effort to get them.

A two-hour class period is, of course, too long to sit still. Years before, when I'd taught one-night-a-week grad seminars (running three hours), I met them in my home near campus, mixing in refreshments along with a half-time break. For this new Intro to Lit course, I could be more inven-tive, based on the strategy of involvement needed for success. First day of class, I'd explain what we would be doing and how it was different. This would be the last time that we'd meet at noon, for example. After sum-marizing what the course was about and taking roll, we'd break up into small groups, groups that after today would spend the first half hour of each session discussing the day's materials. These would form up at the students' discretion, so it would be best to start looking around now for familiar faces or faces they'd like to become familiar with.

"Here's a chance to test your eye contact," I'd tease, letting everyone know from the start that this class was meant to be enjoyed. Another way was to joke about names. I would have written my own, Jerry Klinkowitz,

on the board first thing. Now, as I took out the brand new class list, I'd give the usual cautions about correcting any mispronunciations but would also ask if the registrar was printing out their first names more formally than what they customarily used. "Anybody here get inhibited when they're called 'Robert' rather than 'Bob' or 'Rob,' 'Jennifer' rather than 'Jennie' or 'Jen'?" I'd ask.

Stone cold, nobody usually spoke right up. So I'd go on with an explanation, phrased again as a question.

"Take my name: formally, it's 'Jerome,' but you see I wrote 'Jerry.' Who do you think ever calls me 'Jerome'?"

"Your wife?" a few voices might venture.

"Right," I'd agree. "But only when she's mad at me. Who else?"

"Your mother?" a few more would guess.

"Absolutely!" I'd say this with a smile, then chide them that although they were getting closer, there was someone more obvious who makes you feel bad by using your full first name. This the students would be afraid to answer, though from the growing laughter I could tell everyone knew.

"The *arresting officer*, right?" Over the chuckles and guffaws, I'd go right through the traffic cop routine—"Well, *Jerome,* where's the fire?" and everything. One semester, I had this joke come full circle, as at the end a student who happened to be a graduating senior told me he'd just been accepted into the Iowa Highway Patrol. "If I ever nab you," he assured me, "I'll remember to call you 'Jerry' so you don't feel too badly about it."

During the coming roll call, I'd ask that all pay attention not just to their own names but to everyone else's. Ours would be as much a discussion class as possible, I advised. When I knew something that they didn't, I'd tell them, but as each person's reading was unique, it was part of our work to share these responses. So, learn each other's names.

As for requirements, there were two: discussion and a paper, each counting for half the course grade. No tests? Well, every day was a test of sorts, but I didn't want it to be perceived that way. After all, just getting out of bed in the morning and brushing your teeth was a test, and I had plenty of friends for whom seeing another day dawn was a real victory. Please don't be inhibited by the discussion. Even if you didn't like to talk in class, you had the paper to balance things, and I wouldn't be super strict about the 50–50 grading—show me your strength, and I'd understand. But do try to appreciate that none of you will be spending his or her life writing papers on literature, not even if you bottom out and become a critic like myself!

Here was proof. Had they seen a movie recently, and if so, were all those people filing out from the first show writing papers about it or talking about it? All that talk about stars and themes and music and special effects was why people went to movies: to have something in common to talk about. Facilitating such discussion about artistic endeavor was what this course was meant to do. And to do so, I'd be keeping our practice discussion (as it were) as unthreatening as possible.

Several factors, I'd explain, worked in our favor. Holding up fingers, I'd count them off.

Number one: Our manner would be casually informal. Look at me. Look at how I'm sitting here (in one chair of a double-deep circle), talking like a contemporary American and not an eighteenth-century English lord and dressed not like a bank president but in sport coat, tee-shirt, jeans, and running shoes—a "semiotic code," I'd tell the students, saying that by understanding how styles of dress conveyed messages, they'd already acquired an important critical tool. Wasn't it pretty clear what I was expecting? If in any later classes today they ran into profs wearing power suits and wingtips, they'd know how to handle that, too.

Number two: Our method would be inductive, not deductive. There you go, two more fancy terms; see how smart you are already? Just don't use such terminology here! It's actually a simple matter of realizing that responding to literature isn't a hard science. There is no table of elements, no chemical valences, not even rules and regs as in finance. Instead of one correct answer, to which we'd all work back, there were many—an infinity of correct answers. To find them, we'd approach these writers and their works without preconceptions. Just take note of what there is to see and start putting it together; from our resulting collective intelligence, a hopefully deeper and certainly broader understanding would result.

Number three: Aiding this openness was the nature of who we'd be reading. Not William Shakespeare, Jane Austen, or Herman Melville; for the writers coming up in this course, there were no tried and true approaches as there were for *Hamlet, Pride and Prejudice,* or *Moby-Dick.* This also meant that there was very little they could look up about these authors. What materials there were, I'd mention, but for the most part, we were on our own, because I'd deliberately chosen writers without a critical canon (now you've learned a third term—this is getting good, isn't it?).

Number four: As for the authors we were doing, you didn't have to like them or even think they were very good. I liked them, of course, and

thought their work had merit, but they weren't Shakespeare, Austen, or Melville. The verdict on them was not yet in; the jury was still out, and in this case, our classroom would be a courtroom as well. Was it a problem that some of them were my friends, as may have been noted from blurbs on their books? See point five.

Number five: At no point in this course would anyone be penalized for disagreeing with me. Sure, I knew some profs that did that, and so did any student here who wasn't a first-semester freshman. If anything, my prejudice went the other way: I was most impressed by folks who took a different view from my own, especially when they took the time to support it. After all, that's how knowledge expands. Anybody here play tennis? Handball? Who do you want for an opponent: someone worse than you, or better? As for my friends we'd be reading, I wouldn't be offended if students thought they stank—tell me why, and I'd use it when any of these writers got too uppity with me; as friends, they let me kid them and were always kidding me.

Number six: Now for the small discussion groups. Chances were that this would be the students' most rewarding part of the course. We wouldn't be the first class to use such a format; my idea for it had come from the translation courses my wife was taking for her M.A. in Spanish, where part of each class meeting would be devoted to a breakdown into small work groups. (Today, almost twenty years later, the style is followed across campus, its best successes coming in the School of Business.) For our Intro to Lit course, I could tick off several advantages.

Advantage A: To counter the fact that anyone might feel inhibited speaking up in front of thirty-five strangers, I'd argue that most people felt comfortable in groups of four or five, especially when the three or four others were acquaintances if not friends—or, best of all, allies. That's why we'd choose up small groups and stick with them to the end. Starting with the next class period, I could promise, no one would walk in here alone—vulnerable, naked, afraid—as may have happened this first day. Instead, a student could expect to enter in the company of a tight little group dedicated to a common purpose: making each other look good. Think about it, I'd say—fresh from a thirty-minute prep session among yourselves, you can stride down the hall in knots, pushing others out of your way. Wear gang colors if you want. Seriously, there would be team spirit to this. And speaking of athletic analogies, did anyone here ever play any sport without a decent warmup? Let's use the same technique here, and there won't be any pulled mental muscles or brain cramps. As far as what happens during the

full class meeting, whatever you do, you'll do it stronger, because you will have tried out your ideas and rehearsed your responses among colleagues. Don't worry—if you sound stupid, your friends will tell you; no way will you be laughed at by a roomful of strangers. For each day's class, there will be a question to consider so that as you read, you'll know what to look for, and when you meet, you'll know what to start talking about.

Advantage B: As it would be pandemonium to have all seven or eight groups all meeting here in this one room, please pick another place for your thirty-minute meeting. If your group is coming over from the same dorm or previous-hour building, meet there. Or find an empty classroom here; at such dead hours as noon and three there will be plenty. Or grab a table in the union. Just one request: *don't* meet in a bar on the Hill, even though we can see the drinking strip sitting there just across the lawn from Lang Hall. I don't need a bunch of beer hounds tearing up Tony's and saying, "Hey, we're Jerry Klinkowitz's lit class!" But wherever you meet, it's your turf—I'll visit your group if you want, but that's your option. Just get here by forty minutes past the hour so we can get the larger class underway.

Advantage C: After the small group sessions, we would have a full class, but conducted cooperatively. This was not the kind of course where students would be measured against each other in cutthroat competition. Yes, I knew there were such programs on campus, but this wasn't one of them. Perhaps there was a place for such mandatory washout rates, but not here. Believe me: in the cooperative world of understanding, appreciating, and enjoying literature, the more you helped your colleagues, the more you helped yourself. I wasn't grading on a curve. There were no required Fs and Ds to counterbalance the A's and B's. In this class, students would be graded individually by what they did. I was a tenured full professor, so no administrator could pressure me to deflate grades unfairly. If every single person in the class did A work, I'd turn in thirty-five A's; in all these years of teaching, it hadn't happened yet, but maybe this could be the section that did it.

Number seven: As for the written requirement, that would come as a paper due at the course's end. I'd explain how my own experience taking tests soured me on examinations, especially for a subject such as literature, but if they wished, they could consider the paper as a take-home exam. By looking at the syllabus, they'd see I was suggesting several topics but also encouraging them to devise their own. In either case, the point was to compare and contrast at least two authors on a specific point—how they used women characters, for example, or the extent to which family mat-

ters structured their work, or what role setting played. As for an approach, they should think of the paper as extending class discussion, a matter of coming up with interesting personal interpretations that could be supported by analysis.

Analysis, I knew, was an unfriendly term, redolent of psychiatric treatment and pointy-headed intellectualism, neither of which are of any use to students taking a course like this before setting off on careers in business or industry. So I'd at once start teasing about it, assuring them that this wasn't the introductory course for English majors, Analysis of Literary Forms, which the Scheduling Office computer with uncanny accuracy called "ANAL LIT." Don't worry, I'd assure them, we were not going to do anything like that! But they should realize that they were listening to analysis, and profiting from it, every day. Did they ever watch NFL football? Sure—and how many announcers were there? Yes, two: one for the play-by-play, the other for color. Just think of the difference between Pat Summerall and John Madden, which was the difference between what had happened and why it had happened. Analysis was everywhere, from sports to the stock market report. So, when you write your papers, I'd urge, be sure to set the stage by giving me a little bit of play-by-play, so we'd all know where we were in the story, but as soon as possible switch over to analysis, and let me know how and why and to what consequence the writer was doing what he or she did. Be like John Madden. If waving your arms around helped, do it, but get the analysis done, just like the old Raiders coach with his CBS electronic chalkboard.

Now, just because the paper wasn't due for seven weeks didn't mean all thought for it could be postponed. True, it was October 21 today, in the loveliest part of northeast Iowa's autumn, with the thermometer touching the high sixties, the leaf change in full swing, and afternoons still ripe for sitting barefoot in the grass, soaking up some late slant sun. Papers weren't due 'til December 6, by which time odds were we'd have snow cover out there and be worrying about wind chills on the way to class. That meant the due date would never come, right? Well, you're not going to believe how fast this course will go by, because hopefully, you'll be having a good time.

What everyone should know, I'd emphasize, was that although the finished product probably could be written up in a few hours, this part accounted for less than 5 percent of the task. Most time would be spent *thinking about* the subject—comparative and contrasting thinking that should begin as soon as next week, when we moved from the first to the second of our authors. "These are always the most interesting parts of the course,

at least to me," I'd tell the students, "because they are the interfaces where analysis best happens." But these interfaces come and go quickly. It was their job to put them all together, not just to toss one ball around but juggle two or three of them—if they were brilliant, all four. "Ideas should start popping up right away, so talk them over, jot them down. Notions will change as the course develops—note these changes and ask yourselves why your opinion is now different." I'd explain how a big part of understanding literature is catching on to the flow, both in the work itself and in the reader's growing appreciation of it. "Literature is a living, moving, breathing subject," I'd stress, joking that they should get labels for their book-packs saying, "Caution: Live Animals." Joke or not, from this first introductory class meeting, most students would be thinking about lit texts in a new way.

All this would take about half an hour, during which time the roomful of strangers would have begun to warm up to one another, having shared some common laughs. While still on the subject of papers, I'd tell how this part of the course requirements could tie into the small groups as well. "You might consider," I'd advise, "doing the paper as a group project." This would usually surprise and puzzle the class, so I'd ride that puzzlement for effect.

Don't even think of writing it in common, I'd warn, unless your group was getting along exceptionally well. There'd be no way of telling that for a couple weeks. Not every group would be ideal—if you felt you were getting off to a bad start, let me know, and I'd come by and see what I could do. But as I'd learn after using this format for a few years, some could hit it off well and go on to bigger and better things (one group continued meeting after the course ended just because they liked talking lit, and in another, two of the members, previously unknown to one another, began dating and eventually got married—when I'd mention these examples to subsequent classes, I'd assure them that such behavior was not required). But if it turned out that a group worked well and enjoyed sharing company, then doing a joint paper might be a good idea.

Group papers weren't easier, believe me. They were harder because a quartet of viewpoints would have to be harmonized. Responsibilities could be divided, but this itself was work, too. The only thing easier was not having to face the blank page (or, as the eighties progressed, the blank screen) alone. Yet what could be gained was considerable, including the real-life ability to work in a committee context and help author a report. Here was a good chance to learn how.

Finally, a word on the writers we'd be reading. From semester to semes-

ter, I'd change them and also tinker with my approach. For a while, I did all four genres (including nonfiction prose) spread across different national cultures (at one point even fitting in Roland Barthes, with success). That worked, but not as well as what I tried next: three American fiction writers (Hawthorne, Fitzgerald, and Vonnegut) with a story collection and novel by each. The only reason I abandoned this was because six books in seven weeks were too much; the students were forever reading, and I felt hurried in my coverage—*coverage,* the word that summed up so much of what I felt was wrong with the traditional curriculum for majors. What worked best was presenting four American contemporaries, all of them writing now about things average students would know and in a language they could understand. All would be fictionists, though some were more dramatic, poetic, or expositional than others. I'd emphasize these hints of genre and also use examples of real poems, plays, and essays as they were available by common reference. But the essence was that we read four books— not anthology excerpts but complete works as recently published by living authors, all of them people I knew. The library might not be jammed with commentary on them, but if any students cared, they could drop one or more of them a letter—and many did. Each week, I myself could bring in a postcard or report a phone call, for I was doing work on all of them. So were my students, who grasped the reality of it all completely.

Although I've changed texts most semesters, the most frequently recurring combination has been Stephen Dixon's *14 Stories,* Grace Paley's *Enormous Changes at the Last Minute,* Michael Stephens's *Season at Coole,* and Alice Walker's *In Love and Trouble.* The third is a novel but is structured like a story cycle in its progress through a family, so it served as a good transition from short narratives to long. The story collections themselves are not random but have a mind of their own, so all four books hold together at about the same level of tension: not too tight and not too loose, a balance that's needed for successful teaching.

The same goes for the authors' ages: about the same as mine except for Grace Paley, a lot older, and Michael Stephens, a bit younger. Dixon and Walker were my contemporaries, Paley old enough to be my mother, Stephens the age of a little brother. It really helps to locate one's self some way, and generationally is as good as any, certainly something any student will understand. As far as background, Dixon and Paley were urban, Stephens a kind of ratty down-and-out suburban, and Walker country. *14 Stories* and *Enormous Changes* are mostly (but not exclusively) set in New York City, appropriately enough for the gen ed class because New York was

after all a media capital and familiar to even provincial heartlanders from TV and films. *In Love and Trouble* takes place mostly in the South, but there are some northern contrasts. The ethnicity of *Season at Coole* could happen any place where immigrant traces remain strong among the generations.

Two men, two women. Three religions: Jewish, Catholic, and Protestant, with additional references in Walker's book to African practices and beliefs; two races, black and white, with various minorities making special guest appearances as characters in all four volumes. You couldn't ask for a better mix in current times. All of it was written in a language utterly artistic yet one that I and my students shared, so the subtle variations were apparent: Steve Dixon's jerky, brittle urbanisms; Grace Paley's knowing motherliness; Michael Stephens's full-blown lyricism (he was our poet in prose); and Alice Walker's rhythms and inflections so sympathetic to each character she was exploring.

Having spread things across a much broader generic and national palette before, I knew in my heart that Dixon-Paley-Stephens-Walker gave just as good a sampling of literary topics and techniques, with the advantage that all of it was so basically accessible. It was not a case of dumbing down but rather of taking some extra time to find examples that didn't need twenty minutes of history lessons before you got to the literary art. Images and metaphors and especially analogies were rich in these works, and none of them needed extensive footnoting to work their magic on the reader. In this already much too busy world, we could stop dithering around and get right to the crucial point, which was how these texts functioned.

For the first day's class, which had now run about forty minutes, one last matter of business remained: explaining how as a Monday-Wednesday-Friday class we would indeed meet on Fridays—yes, even late Friday afternoon, when we'd probably be the only sentient life on campus. I knew that this was the University of Northern Iowa, where weekends began at 4:00 P.M. on Thursday. Even a noon class on Friday could be a problem. I knew people had rides home to catch. I knew they had jobs. And yes, there was going to be the occasional illness or (God forbid) tragedy to attend to. Other courses sometimes had out-of-town trips to take, not to mention intercollegiate athletics. Listen: everybody is going to miss a class or two for good reason. But given this fact, please don't blow off a bunch of Fridays on top of that. As a half-semester double-time course, one day's missed class was like two. And because discussion was so important, you just couldn't afford to lose continuity. Fall one step behind, and it could be all hell to recover.

But don't worry—I could offer two strategies for making Fridays more workable. For one thing, on the three occasions when full class meetings weren't required (for considering, organizing, and finally drafting group papers, when continuing with fresh readings would be distracting), I'd make sure these days fell on Fridays; if you had to be away then, have your group meet before or after. Second, on the few Fridays we did meet, attendees would be rewarded with a joke, starting the end of this week with the Famous Talking Dog Joke. Just saying this usually got laughs, and I'd build on them by chiding how this was probably the reason so many here today had signed up for the course. As it would happen, my jokes were an important part of learning how to understand and critique literature, but that wouldn't become apparent 'til the end, and I didn't want the fun spoiled by revealing the trick now. So I made it seem like Friday's first joke would be a real doozy. Okay, get ready to choose up groups and decide where you're going to meet Wednesday and every class day hereafter. But take this question with you, which you'll also find on the syllabus: in the stories from Steve Dixon's book that we'll discuss, "Streets" and "The Signing," consider what kind of guy the narrator is and how these personality traits help create each story's predicament. Don't go looking for symbols or fancy bits of psychoanalysis—just treat the narrator like someone you've met and who's talking to you. Size him up, decide if you trust him, try to figure out what's going on. "Don't you know some people who create their own problems?" I'd ask. "Use those skills here."

Two days later, the class would reassemble, but as promised, the mood was different. Students arrived in clusters instead of separately, and their happy chatter continued as the room filled and I jotted some data on the board. Nothing about Stephen Dixon yet. I wanted to hear the students' reactions before letting biography influence perceptions. Taking my seat in the double circle, I'd project as open a mind as possible, and for good reason: the two Dixon stories up for discussion were nothing like these people had ever read in a high school language arts class.

"So—what do you think of this guy?" I'd ask, and would almost always get a bevy of responses. For the rare class where timidity kept things quiet, I'd prod them with something personal, along the lines of, "Hey, the guy who wrote this book is one of my best friends on Earth, and sometimes he acts just like the guys in his stories. Would you want a friend like this?" The key was letting the class know that they were welcome to start considering these stories personally, the same way they'd talk about somebody

new from a dorm lounge, bar, or party. After all, stories were written with a response in mind.

Steve Dixon's narrator in "Streets" is an easy and obvious study. In trying to do well, he winds up doing worse, and rapid-fire examples would make our first literary discussion shoot off like a string of firecrackers. From here, I'd ask about the language being used—any correlations? This wouldn't be as easy, so we'd have to focus on something quite simple: the story's first line. Anything unusual about it? Well, it's a simple declarative sentence, written in the present tense, but that's all. How about the second one. Aha! It's another declarative sentence, but this time retracting the information given in the first. Pretty different from "Once upon a time there was . . . ," isn't it? Look how our experience changes for Steve's story: instead of being given historic fact, we're presented with an event as it happens, and none too clearly at that. Make you feel uncertain about it, insecure? Now you know how the narrator feels, worrying that he's going to mess up.

From here, we'd go on to the next obvious point, and not just in the story's action. Yes, the sentences give information, then retract it. What about the paragraphs? Nothing fancy, just look at them physically. I'd hold the book at arm's length, too far away to read the words, but letting the physical nature of the print take better shape. See, there it is: long, fat paragraphs alternating with skinny ones. Why does Steve do this? What happens in the thick sections? The narrator describes what's happening. And then in the thin ones? The crowd around him argues with his account. Even more destabilizing, right? But at least there's variation, a rhythm to things, which is always pleasurable. Imagine what it would be like if the entire story were one long, dense paragraph? Yes, boring. But would having it be all lines of very short dialogue be any better? No, too scattered. The rhythm does make sense.

Look what we'd have underway here in this supposedly bonehead gen ed lit course: a technical discussion about the physical nature of the story, concentrating on the art with which it was made, all after just a few introductory comments on the presumed human action. So what should be difficult about this? In their own majors, my engineering students would study how machines work, and my finance students learn how accounting techniques held together and added up. All I was doing was inviting them to handle literature the same way.

The pedagogy is simple but essential: have your students realize from the start that when encountering a narrative, they're responding quite natu-

rally to the way it's made and not just to the action it represents. Steve Dixon's example in "Streets" is a plain, simple one, but from it, we'd move right to a somewhat more complicated example, his "The Signing." As a transition, I'd ask how "Streets" ended. Was anything accomplished? Just more trouble, in ways that made it seem the narrator's problematics would go on forever (the penultimate scene replicates the opening one). So then, how does it end? The only way possible: the narrator closes his eyes, making further reports impossible.

So now, in this shorter, second story, do you see anything happening that gives it the shape it has? What about the first line: "My wife dies. Now I'm alone. I kiss her hands and leave the hospital room" (54). Is that a very promising opening? Sounds more like the end to a narrative. So why doesn't it end? Easy: *because the people in and around the hospital won't let it.* The doctor, the nurse, the guard in the lobby, the driver of the bus—all do their best to constrain the poor man, who only wants to grieve alone. Look right across the page: when he's first stopped, he repeats the story's first line, verbatim, as if he's trying for the proper cue. Let's *end!* So all the things that happen—which are pretty ridiculous, when you think about it—make sense as a resistance to what he's trying to do, which is make the story conclude. When it finally does, has anything changed? Yes: the narrator's injury brings him back to the hospital, where he's not only treated (in the same room where he'd first brought his wife) but is guided through the motions of signing the papers for her body, the act he'd been resisting since the start. Rules are rules, and until they are satisfied, the story can't end—another mechanical ending, just like the first.

Discussion would follow about all the rules and regs in the piece, not just for the narrator but as governing the acts of medical staff, security, even communications and transport. How silly, right, that people let themselves be so controlled? Of course. But did you notice anything special? What gender is the doctor? Ah—female. And the nurse? Male! So why should you notice that? Because Steve is playing a little trick on us, showing how outdated rules and regulations still govern our supposedly nonsexist thought.

With our first full class meeting coming to an end, I'd ease back and ask if the class would like something nice: did they want to hear a story? Everyone loves a story, and this would be one they didn't have to analyze, just enjoy. (Fat chance! They'd just spent an hour being brilliant analysts and savoring every moment of it.) The story, "Favorites," was written by a friend of both mine and Steve's, Robley Wilson, who thought he could do an even better job with the nature of grief. I'd spin out the plot leisurely

but emphasize the climax, which comes after the narrator's wife dies suddenly and is buried, leaving him to continue life alone.

"The night of her funeral, neighbors bring the man some dinner. But as he puts away the leftovers, he sees something surprising in the refrigerator: a chocolate pie his wife had baked for him the day she died. It was her specialty and his favorite, the secret for which would have died with her. He wonders what to do with the pie. What would you do?"

"Freeze it."

"Eat it."

"Throw it out—it would just make him too sad to eat a piece, knowing that it was the last one ever."

"There you go," I'd say, indicating the route to Rob's solution. As it happens, the guy eats a piece, enjoying the great taste and also having happy memories about what a wonderful woman his wife was. Next night, he has another piece, and so on for a week, until there's just one left. So, what does he do? What would *you* do?"

"Snarf it"

"Freeze it."

"Nope," I'd say and describe how he cut it in half, leaving the rest. Next night, he'd cut the half in half, eating a quarter piece. Night after that, he'd cut the quarter in half, eating an eighth, and so on, until there was just a razor-thin slice of it left, barely enough to stand up.

"And then what does he do? You can see physically that the story's ending; this is the last page, just a line of print left. Can you guess?"

Someone would, correctly: he eats the last bite, and the story ends.

Yeah, pretty cute. But when you think about it, the story says a lot about grief, coming to terms with loss, and getting on with the rest of your life. Grief itself is very hard to talk about, and too often misguided attempts degenerate into sentimentality and bathos. Robley Wilson doesn't let that happen here because he uses a correlative for grief. It's hard to write about the widower's feelings but easy to write about the pie, especially when its slices have a structure of their own, just the structure we lack for pure grief. But when we're with the pie, we know something about that grief, don't we?

Same thing for "The Signing," right?

For the next class, I'd ask my students to read two more of Steve's stories, "The Security Guard" and "Out of Work." I'd also say to go ahead and read some of the other pieces in *14 Stories* we weren't covering, any that looked interesting, except for one: "Milk Is Very Good for You." This would be a joke, of course. They'd ask why not, and I'd ask in return why

they couldn't tell from the nasty title how objectionable the story was. They'd laugh about reverse psychology, and I'd protest even more. By day's end, most students would have read the story and got the joke: that it is probably the dirtiest tale ever written, yet without a single sexual-reference word in it—all such mentions are in nonsense language but obvious nevertheless, making any perceived dirtiness the reader's doing rather than the author's, a good technique to spot early on. I'd also promised that because the class was on Friday afternoon, attendance would be rewarded with a joke, the Famous Talking Dog Joke. So by the time Friday rolled around, things had been loosened up considerably from all the challenges faced on Monday, challenges reaching from starting a new class to wondering if this new methodology could be trusted.

For these two new stories, the question would be a development from the previous class: after having considered how the narrator's personality creates the predicament in "Streets" and "The Signing," how does the nature of the job generate the complications in "The Security Guard" and "Out of Work"? You'd be surprised how many students have worked as security guards in some way—a few as actual rent-a-cops, more for event security, a couple as bouncers in the local college bars on the Hill, and two guys as Military Police and Shore Patrol. Beyond this, many in the class had worked in retail sales and dealt with the type of shoplifting problems Steve describes. So even before moving into the story, it would be easy to get discussion going. The bouncer from Joker's and the navy vet had great stories themselves, and I could tell my own from the ballpark, where for opening day we'd briefed the new security team about breaking up fights, not realizing that when we meant fights in the stands, they were thinking of fights on the field. It was quite a scene when during the inevitable brushback brawl the sea of churning white and gray uniforms was peppered with the brown of Guardian Security, something for which we had to answer to the League.

The point from this flurry of responses would be that by the very nature of the job, a security guard does not command the respect that a police officer does. Combined with the fact that Steve's narrator only takes the job as a last resort, trouble is almost guaranteed to happen. The specific problem revolves around his use of the club. There will be times when he's expected to use it, and he's not sure that he can. How early in the story do you know there's going to be trouble? Certainly from the second page, where after the narrator's admission that he's been out of work a long time, he applies for this unsuitable job and endures a four hundred-word expla-

nation of his duties (all in a solid block paragraph) with just one question on his mind: "Hit with a club you mean?" (60).

After our opening small talk about how tough the job is, students are ready for something technical: how by now we've learned that when Steve hits us with one of these massive, page-filling paragraphs, we're not expected to follow it like Gospel— indeed, trying to keep track of the complicated, complex, and sometimes contradictory instructions would give you a headache, as it's probably doing to his hapless narrator who can only think of one thing, the requirement that he be able to hit someone with his club. How do we know this? Does he say so? Not exactly, because the narrator is evasive enough to bluff his way through the interview and get hired. The answer for us as readers is textual, plainly obvious from that massive block of interviewer prose that elicits such a pipsqueak response.

At this point, I'd talk a bit, telling the students something they probably didn't know: the principle of literary composition deriving from Henrik Ibsen's *Hedda Gabler*. Ibsen and his role in modern drama could be explained in half a minute, the stage set and opening exposition in a minute and a half. Yes, right in the middle of all this womanly politeness is something hanging there on the wall like the world's most monumental distraction: two big hulking guns. What are they doing there? Right, you've got to be asking yourself this, and it's not long before an explanation comes, all about Hedda's father and who he was and how the guns remain as a tribute to him, odd as they look among the more prevalent signs of middle-class femininity. Yes, a plot develops, and Hedda's character is gradually revealed to have aggressive tendencies. But the point here is a simple one, applicable to any number of subsequent literary works, including "The Security Guard": if there's a gun hanging on the wall at the start of act 1, you can bet it's going to be fired by the end of act 3.

Students would grasp this immediately: Ibsen's gun is Dixon's club, the examples working all the better because both are personal weapons. And they could also show me how, just as in Hedda's case, the weapon isn't used until the very end. Most important, they'd appreciate how the weapon's presence would loom over the action, all this time—we'd tick off the three incidents in which Steve's narrator does *not* use the club, always making things worse for himself. By doing this, the students were involving themselves in the story on a technical level, taking what didn't make a lot of sense in terms of simple plot summary and instead telling me how these conditions of employment were generating the action, action which by itself seemed ridiculous. They all had jobs and knew the hassles, telling me

how flipping the burgers was the least of it. Now, they could apply this insight, one they'd already learned the long and hard way, to the mechanics of fictive narrative. I'd ask them if the narrator's eventual use of the club, when he stops a likely rapist from getting past him to a woman, makes us feel happy with how things end.

No, we don't, and the reason why goes right back to the start. He's the wrong person for the job, and no amount of even heroic behavior can change that. The club, like Hedda's gun, has to be used before he and we know that to total satisfaction. By putting it off, an interesting action has resulted, one that says much about the travails of security work. Certainly, enough interest is stimulated and attention maintained, all of it letting Dixon as author engineer some remarkable occurrences. Everything happens just the right way so that the story is technically as well as situationally convincing. Reading "The Security Guard" with these points in mind is a good way of learning how fiction works.

"The Security Guard" leads naturally to "Out of Work," for while students in the class have either been involved with security duties themselves or have had a friend who's done such, it is their teacher who can relate to the narrator's predicament in this new story: interviewing for a faculty appointment. Here is where I'd take some time to get into Steve's biography, remarking that after having been born in New York City in 1936, he didn't get his first serious long-term developing job until 1980. How would you like that, I'd ask: start looking for something at graduation and not settle on your career track until age forty-four? Yes, there had been false starts, trying to fulfill his father's wish by taking the required predental school courses in college but not being able to hack the science, then graduating with expertise in political science and journalism but not liking the style of work that followed. What did Steve like, and what was he good at? Sure, writing fiction, but it's darned hard earning a living at that. So for two decades he took day jobs, dozens of them, everything from bartending and restaurant managing and acting to working at Macy's Department Store in retail sales. Was he a security guard? I'd have to ask him, but I'll bet he at least did something like it, as his story reads so knowledgeably. Did he ever apply for teaching positions at schools like the mythical college in "Out of Work" before landing his present and stable position at Johns Hopkins University? Of course. Is this story true? Well, Steve had told me how he had to make up much of the stuff we'd read because the truth was unbelievable, which is precisely what you're supposed to do when crafting good fiction.

"Out of Work" is one of those made-for-teaching stories, as it's funny as all get out and nicely suited to diagramming on the chalkboard. Once again, the narrator is scraping the bottom of the barrel when he applies, and at a great disadvantage because his experience has been as a working actor rather than as a university careerist. He's a dyed-in-the-wool New Yorker; the school is in northeastern South Dakota—rural environs, jerk-water town, hell-hole of a faculty community, and so forth. So anybody with any sense knows this really shouldn't be happening, only the worst can come of it. But it *is* happening, and even though we know what's going to come, there will surely be some fun getting there, as from the start Steve makes it clear the occasion has been one sick (but still hilarious) joke. Progress through the recruitment and interview visit is easy to chart. Drawbacks mount, including the position's shrinkage from three years to one, its increase in duties, and its haplessness for any intelligent person among such a wretchedly incompetent staff (the jibes at boorish professor behavior would test one's credibility were they not so true, as any students beyond their first semester here would have noted). During his interview visit, the narrator is not only given worse and worse horrors to see but is systematically humiliated. Never just one slight, but several in a row, each compounding the hurt—the best example is how he's asked to give a presentation pro bono and then admission is charged so that subsequent visitors can be paid! Believe me, students have a great time listing the atrocities, all of which I remind them are credible because the narrator doesn't know the proper drill and is hence taken advantage of so ridiculously.

Why then does he stick it out? Easy, as graphing the narrative project shows. As the value of the job deteriorates, his chances of getting it improve, so he hangs on to the end. And what a perfect ending it is. There's no surprise that he isn't hired, and it's probably better that he remains in New York—even one year out there in that department from hell might have killed him. But degradations continue right to the end, as he (correctly) declines to cash what he considers an insufficient travel reimbursement only to have it bounce when he does give up, leaving him out everything plus responsible for a bad check fee.

Now for the Talking Dog Joke. By this time, I would have made such a big deal of it that people had to know it was a stinker—the same reverse psychology that had them off reading "Milk Is Very Good for You" when I'd told them not to. Why does one tell a deliberately bad joke? To sharpen listeners' critical skills, that's why. Today and for the other Fridays when we'd meet, I'd tell one of these, making fun of how corny they were—

building up a predictable rhythm, which at the very end of the semester I'd bring to a climax, as will be noted. For the record, here's how the Talking Dog Joke, learned from my friend Kurt Osborn when I was in second grade, goes.

A guy walks into a bar and sits down on a barstool. Right behind him comes a dog, who takes a seat on the barstool beside him. You can tell they're together because the guy's wearing a blue stocking cap, the dog's wearing a blue stocking cap. The bartender comes over and says, "Get this mutt out of here!" The guy says, "Hey, this is no mutt, this is the famous talking dog." The bartender says, "I don't care if he can sing and dance, too, get him out of here!" The guy says, "Hey, I really mean it, he can talk, and I can prove it—I'll even bet you ten dollars." The bartender agrees, saying he'll be glad to pocket ten bucks before tossing the dog out, and turns to listen.

"Spot," the guy says—that's the dog's name, Spot—"what's on top of a house?" The dog looks up, takes a breath, and says "Roof!"

This brings the bartender halfway over the bar, grabbing the ten dollar bill and reaching for the dog's collar. "Hey, wait!" the guy pleads. "That was ambiguous. This is a sports bar; let me ask my dog a sports question, okay? Double or nothing!" The bartender agrees, reminding himself that taking twenty bucks will be twice the fun before this mutt goes flying. He turns again to listen.

"Spot," the guy says, "Who was the greatest New York Yankees outfielder of all time?" The dog looks up, takes a breath, and says, "Ruth!"

This does it. The bartender's over the bar, pocketing the other ten and grabbing the dog with one hand and the guy with the other to boot them out the door.

There the guy is, sprawled in the gutter. There's Spot next to him, trying to shake off all the muck into which they've been thrown. The guy gives Spot a withering look. Spot looks back, genuinely offended, and says, "So who was I supposed to say, Joe Dimaggio?"

Next Monday, as veterans of four Steve Dixon stories and one bad joke, we'd reassemble to discuss "14 Stories" and "Love Has Its Own Action." These are two of the volume's most complex stories and would have been murder to begin with. But after all these hours of discussion, students could be trusted to catch on to Steve's techniques, especially when the stories were almost nothing but technique, so thoroughly does their content resist rationalization as believable subject matter. To make sure the class knew this, I'd phrase the preparation question more obviously than usual: At which

points does each narrative's action regenerate itself and go on to the next stage, a stage that by itself might not necessarily follow?

"14 Stories" is the title piece to Steve's collection, a volume that in fact contains just thirteen of his short narratives. Did anyone notice? Are there any other deviations from a conventional count to fourteen? Yes, floor thirteen is skipped in the hotel's numbering, a nod to superstition that you sometimes find on airplanes as well with the rows going from twelve to fourteen, with nothing in between. Are we ourselves superstitious? Of course not. But like Steve's trick with the medical sexism, it shows us that we at least noticed.

More important, the business with numbers alerts readers that Steve is playing with the idea of more than one story line. Are there fourteen of them in "14 Stories"—or, perhaps, thirteen? There's certainly not just one, for the initial narrative is over almost before it starts: "Eugene Randall held the gun in front of his mouth and fired. The bullet smashed his upper front teeth, left his head through the back of his jaw, pierced an ear lobe and broke a window that overlooked much of the midtown area" (1). Just like "The Signing," it sounds like the end to a conventional tale. Here, again, it's the start. But with a twist, as the narrator pays so much attention to the bullet's path. From here, students would suggest why: initially because the story's next stage involves this same bullet hitting a wall next to a terrified kid several blocks away, while the one after that involves a couple finding Eugene Randall's suicide note after it has drifted out the broken window. The sound of the gunshot is overheard elsewhere, always misunderstood, just as are the wounded man's gaspings into the phone. That one act, meant to be his last, has in fact initiated a dozen others, all of them equally confused. It almost seems that Steve is trying to stretch things as far as he can.

Can the structure bear it? Just barely, students would answer. More than once, I'd have an industrial technology student point out that the density of examples in "Streets" and "The Signing" let Dixon distribute his materials across a broad expanse, whereas here he was stringing things as lightly as possible—a suspension bridge or Eiffel Tower, say, rather than a pyramid or block building.

"So," I'd ask, "is he doing this just as a demonstration, just showing off? Or is there some other point to it?"

"It teaches you not to commit suicide," I'd be told. "It's a good lesson about how you really can't 'end it all.'"

"It also tells you how communication breaks down," another student

would add. "The note, the phone, the sound of the shot—those are all messages that get mixed up."

"What about the bullet?" I'd tease. "Is that a message?"

"Depends on what kind of neighborhood you live in," someone would laugh, and I'd agree. But the point was well made, that nothing happened in "14 Stories" without occasioning something else, until it all ends with the hotel maid having to clean up, asking, "Why me?"

Our second story would be an even better example of Steve's self-generative technique. "Love Has Its Own Action" seems preposterous when you simply consider its represented action, which involves the narrator running through a long series of affairs in which women are dropped for others at the drop of a hat, or less. Without preparation, readers might think this was overtly sexist. But in light of my initial question and the discussion we'd had with "14 Stories," this new piece would seem less a disquisition on sex than another exercise in stretching the limits of structure.

"What are the essential components of structure, anyway?" I'd ask a design major. "Time and space—and how they're utilized in creating the final form," she'd answer.

"Anything done with time and space here, in Steve's story?"

Again, examples would come left and right. The first episode is conventional, the romance developing normally and at ease. How does it end? The woman jilts the man. After that, he drops every woman with whom he starts a relationship—each time more quickly, each time with less and less provocation, until near the end the switches are coming at us not just every page, not just every paragraph, but in almost every line.

Okay, that's the structure, an increasing acceleration. But what about the substance? How are these relationships, increasingly quick as they are, described?

"They're always the best and happiest ever," someone would venture. "The women are always the most beautiful, most wonderful, most loving he's ever met, one after another!"

Were there any foreign language majors here who could tell me the grammatical name for such qualifications?

"Superlatives," I'd be told. "Adjectives have three states: normative, comparative, and superlative. As in *good, better,* and *best.*"

"Yes indeed!" I'd agree then ask if there were any normatives or comparatives in this story, in this world Steve describes.

"No," would come the answer. "So I guess he doesn't have any choice but to go on, as whatever's next is always the best."

Was anyone surprised by the ending? You bet. With heterosexual affair after affair running pell mell through the story at an ever-increasing pace, the action promises to go on to an unmeasurable infinity well beyond the speed of reading—*always measure your own response,* I'd remind. And so Dixon engineers a binary shift, having the narrator hitch a ride with a truck driver, another male, with whom he begins something entirely different. The ending isn't antigay, nor is it progay, just as the preceding affairs have not been degrading of women. While individually, the episodes could be credible, Steve's way of stringing them together isn't. The sex certainly isn't—not unless you're Beavis and Butthead. For the sake of any randy fourteen year olds who might read it, perhaps the story should carry a product warning: do not try this at home. So then why is all this nonsense there? To highlight the textual action, to remind us that what we're reading is not in life but on the page, which is to where we must direct our attention. Just like the endings of Steve's first two stories, how else is the heterosexual action to stop?

So the tricks are not for their own sake but to prevent us from reading this story the wrong way and get us on track to see the art. But it would be unfair to Steve Dixon and unwise pedagogy to let coverage end on the level of technique alone. Yes indeed, this author is a master of such technical aspects, but he has produced stories packed with human meaning and deep feeling as well. In preparation for our last pair, "The Sub" and "Ann from the Street," I'd tell the class about Steve's life, focusing on all those unattached years before he got hired to teach in the Writing Seminars at Johns Hopkins University and shortly after married a professor of Russian at Hopkins, Anne Frydman. These were the years, during the middle seventies, when I met Steve and visited him several times in New York City. What was his life like back then? Well, fiction is never autobiography, but I could guess that there was an autobiographical flavor to the integrated pieces collected in the book published just a year before *14 Stories,* a volume called *Quite Contrary: The Mary and Newt Story,* in which a couple's consistency of relationship is that they're always breaking up. What was Steve doing for these twenty-some years before being taken on at Hopkins? Just about everything, from writing copy for radio journalism to editing detective magazines, working as a bartender, clerking at Macy's Department Store, and substitute teaching. Aha—is "The Sub" autobiographical, and is Anne Frydman the woman in "Ann from the Street"? No way; fiction is not that simple, and besides, Steve had not yet met this particular Anne when he wrote the latter story. But given all that, the immen-

sity of emotion in both pieces implies there's at least some of the author present, and to find out just how, please try to determine just where the narrative in each changes levels—shifts gears, modulates, takes on a different tone, whatever.

There are dozens of Steve Dixon stories with a narrator similar to the one in "The Sub." In his midthirties, career not yet on track, doing something to tide things over, he still lives at home with his parents, including a sick father whom he helps his mother nurse—a dutiful, sincere, but very lonely personality type that Dixon has mined again and again for a richness of sensitivity. "The Sub" would let us see how such a narrator's fantasizing about an attractive woman creates an entire, if artificial, existence—which even after the woman denies it keeps being generated by virtue of the narrator's change of verb mood, from declarative to optative and subjunctive.

"Just look how they pepper the last two pages," I'd say, holding up my book to show off the encircled words: *should, would, could, might,* and so forth. "Shouldda-wouldda-couldda," I'd repeat, "what a sad state in which to live. And that's how he keeps it going, though he does admit that the woman it will happen with probably won't be her."

"But all his projections sound so lovely," a student would offer. "The marriage, the honeymoon in Europe, all those café au laits in little bistros, the big feather beds . . . "

"I agree," I'd say. "But don't worry. It was right after this that Steve met Anne, they fell in love and got married and had exactly this type of honeymoon!" Is this Anne the real Steve Dixon married the character in "Ann from the Street"? A good question, but the answer is no. Look at the immediate evidence, right in the title: the names are spelled differently, and the fictive woman is drawn as someone the narrator has known for years, an old friend from the neighborhood, his block, his street. Plus, in the narrative, she'd had a full life for the past ten or fifteen years, including career, marriage, and now about to have a baby, while the narrator reflects that he has nothing. As their momentary meeting ends and she leaves, he tries to keep her there in his story, but it all fades out: "She walks. Is so pretty. Voice face smile niceness kindness lovingness warmth" (125), the sentence itself decomposing. Then, she herself moves out of easy view, leaving sentence number two with no subject. Finally, just abstract qualities remain, syntax itself deconstructing once there is nothing left to represent. Tricky, right? But only because there's more to come, when with reality depleted the narrator shifts levels to fantasy.

"I picture her coming home to me," he says, and what a beautifully crafted scene it is, as lovely as the imagined honeymoon in "The Sub." But here, the shift just makes him and us feel worse. Look how it's done, as he pictures the two of them so happy that they decide to make love:

> I could even lift her up and carry her but that might scare her so I don't think I would. Later she might say or before we get into bed that she met someone I know on the street. I'd say "Who?" and she'd say "You. I said I'd give you your regards. No, you said to give you your best and I said I'd tell you I saw you on the street." (125)

As simple as drawing a circle, Dixon lets his narrator project himself out of relatively bearable isolation into a context filled with everything he lacks, only to have the very structure of its language (which is rhymed for effect) deposit him back there on the street, all alone, once more on the outside looking in—and all the more lonely for having been inside for that little bit. We as readers feel separation because it has happened not just as a portrayed event (the story's first level) but also as an accomplishment of language. Look how far we've come with Steve Dixon since "Streets" and "The Signing": still some grammatical tricks and plenty of literary art, but an immensity of meaning and feeling as well.

In finishing up our four classes on Dixon's work, I'd complete his biography, describing how despite his late start (or maybe because of it, in gratitude) he'd become the world's best husband, father, and university creative writing professor. Did he write happier stories about these new roles now? Yes, but with a twist. I'd summarize one of them from his early years of parenthood, about how a guy, middle-aged and single, walks past an open window and sees a man inside holding a baby in his arms and dancing with it as if to the music of inestimable joy. This vision inspires the guy to get his own life on track, working to meet someone nice for a change and sticking with her, getting married, and eventually having a child. As the story comes to an end, there he is, holding the little baby just brought home and dancing in delight—at which point he sees a stranger looking in the window and quickly pulls the curtains shut, so no one will see. Then, another story from when Steve's daughters were little kids, about a man taking his small child to the beach and inexplicably losing her. Finally, a summary of a third one, more recently written, of a marriage failing. Had Steve ever lost one of his kids? Were things with Anne on the rocks? No way; everything with his daughters and his wife was fine. But these were

any person's fears, that things wanted for so long and finally achieved could be lost. Don't worry—his daughters were in their midteens now; they weren't going to get lost on the beach, and although Anne had suffered some health problems, Steve had become an even better husband in response. But fears are fears and as properties of the imagination were great generators of stories. *Powerful* generators indeed; if you have any doubts, read Steve's novel *Interstate,* which tells a similar horrific story seven different ways before rewarding readers with an eighth version, whose otherwise banal well-being is treasured all the more for what could have happened but finally hasn't.

For Friday's class, there would be two preparations: read Grace Paley's story "Samuel" and be ready for the Famous Platypus Joke. Both were good reasons to attend. "Samuel," students may have noted, was scarcely three and a half pages long. What was this Famous Platypus Joke, something that would take the better part of an hour to tell? No—even though we'd been whipping through two Steve Dixon stories per class, stories that averaged a dozen pages each, Grace Paley was a different style of author, one given to more poetic use of language from time to time, and therefore more space should be allowed for considering her work. By all means, don't leave the piece unread until five minutes before your group meeting, as that would make for much frustration. Grace was up to some pretty interesting things in this story, and you'd probably want to read the pages slowly, giving them some thought—there'd be no razzle-dazzle tricks or pratfall comedy as in some of the earlier Dixon stuff we'd read. Grace was older, more serious from the get-go, more pointed in what she wanted to say, more . . . Well, you'd see soon enough. But as a guide to reading "Samuel," brief as it is, and also to emphasize the fact that we'd be changing writers, consider this: Is there anything in the way this story is told that suggests it was written by a woman?

At the start of Friday's class, I'd confess my own special interest, how these were the most exciting parts of the course for me, because they were the momentary interfaces when we were passing from one author to another. I was really intrigued by what these first-time readers of Stephen Dixon thought as they took their initial look at something by Grace Paley. Trusting that I'd want honest first impressions, the students would volunteer them gladly. She's slower, they'd say. Less jerky, less frantic than Steve's narrators. Easier to keep track of. And, as I'd warned them, more serious. This was great: not yet two full weeks into the analysis of literature, and they were already responding to the story according to its language. Yes,

Grace uses words differently, I'd agree, adding that in subsequent assign-
ments they'd be seeing situations where the action made sense most of all
in terms of language. As for matters being represented, this wasn't just
gossip, but gossip *with an art*. Surely, they had friends who were more
convincing because of the spin they put on things, masters of the body
English thus applied to what might otherwise be plain American speech.
In Paley's stories, there would be lots of this to come, but there was some
of it here, too, even in this very short short story.

If you hadn't seen Grace's name on the book's cover, would you suspect
"Samuel" was written by a woman? Right at the start, on page 103, there's
a pretty good clue. "Some boys are very tough," we're told. "They're afraid
of nothing. They are the ones who climb a wall and take a bow at the top,"
and so on for an introductory paragraph of generalities. Isn't it true that
when somebody generalizes about a group, chances are the person isn't a
member of that group? You know: people talking about things like the
Japanese work ethic, the sense of determination in Israel, the get-ahead
spirit of young Irish people seeking work in the European Union or United
States—even when the generalization is positive, such blanket-statement
making usually comes from an outside perspective. Maybe that's the first
clue. Others follow in short order, as the generalities narrow down to specifics, from "some boys" to four of them (and one in particular, Samuel),
and from all sorts of bravado behavior to one special kind, jiggling on the
swaying platform between subways cars in motion (note the transition
word between paragraphs one and two, *jiggle,* that takes us from generalities to specifics). People in the subway car who notice this behavior are
classed by gender, with the men tending to laugh it off, the women showing concern. Not that either group is effective in warding off danger. From
Paley's introductory manner and strategy of focus, you *know* something
bad is going to happen, and (from the title) to whom.

Throughout, there are subtle touches of gender-based reaction. If men
in the car do worry for a moment, they soon remember their own high
jinx from boyhood days and discount the risk. Some of the women knit
their brows, as if a scowl will shame the boys into better behavior. Others
worry about being sassed if they speak up and blushing. A few suspect that
these kids' mothers don't know where they are. Wrong! Their mothers do,
for the boys are returning from a class trip to see an army missile exhibit
on Fourteenth Street. (Prompting their aggressive behavior, I'd add—
Grace, as a lit professor herself, was teasing English majors everywhere with
such an obvious phallic symbol).

What I'd want my class to see—beyond phallic symbols, of course—was how Grace's careful choice of language both tips off the gender question and motivates the story's action. It comes when one man—a sissy type himself when back in school—finds himself so annoyed that he takes matters into his own hands. Specifically, he pulls the emergency brake (meant to be used only to prevent the train from leaving a station such as when someone might be stuck in a door), causing such a sudden deceleration that Samuel is thrown to his death.

Examining the man's motivation could make for a gossipy discussion, so I'd ask instead if there were anything unusual about how his action was described. Well, a student would venture, it says he gets up to act in a "citizenly" way. Not a strange word, but not your usual diction, either. We'd consider the implications of *citizenly* in this context and suspect Grace was making a judgment, faulting him as a headstrong, take-charge guy who was acting without thought to consequence.

Is there anywhere else in the story where Grace uses such exceptional language? No—not even in the death scene, which happens in just a few flat phrases, less than a dozen words. As for reaction, we must wait until the end, when Samuel's mother is given the terrible news. Before that, we wonder why no one else has screamed, even as we've seen the accident coming from the start and wanted to scream out against it ourselves. But that privilege is reserved for the bereaved mother, whose scream, once released, continues on into an infinite future, a future that can never replace her lost child.

With this first story by Grace Paley, I was taking the class to a new style of appreciation. Steve Dixon's stories offered abundant details for rewarding discussion and structural devices that invited even the most naive reader to play along and see how the narrative was being made. Turning to Grace, my students would find an author comparatively stingy with details and rather tight-lipped about the keys to her structure. Her manner was, as we could all see, more subtle. Without obvious signs, we'd have to attend to little nuances she was introducing by using an unexpected word. Why? What did it connote? How would the story be different if she'd said it more plainly? Not that her first story lacked action: geez, someone was killed, a child, losing his life not so much from his own childishness as from the immaturity of a supposedly responsible adult. "Samuel" had taken us on an emotional roller coaster, and as we'd learned about emotions from "The Signing" and Rob Wilson's "Favorites," a writer had to be really careful here, as Grace most definitely was.

Emotional wringers, for me, called for relief. Plus, it would be Friday now, so time for a joke. As advertised, it was something I called the Famous Platypus Joke. Anybody here know what a platypus is? Of course you do, and there would always be plenty of volunteers to describe the duck-billed platypus, zoologically famous as an egg-laying mammal. Where is it found? Australia. But listen, there will still be educational value to this joke, you'll learn something you didn't know. Take this situation: you've got a zoo director whose board of trustees wants him to establish a platypus exhibit. You know what a zoo director is and how smart they are, right? Remember Marlon Perkins hosting *Mutual of Omaha's Wild Kingdom* every Sunday night? Well, in real life, he was a zoo director, director of the St. Louis Zoo, and he was pretty sharp: anytime there was anything dangerous, like a school of vicious piranha ready to shred him to bits, he'd say, "While Jim heads upstream . . . " and segue to a commercial, where he'd sell parents some term life and catastrophic health insurance (with which Jim was presumably covered). Okay, so you can picture stately old Marlon Perkins down in his office at the St. Louis Zoo, getting ready to e-mail the National Zoo of Australia. He gets on the net and starts typing: "Dear National Zoo of Australia, please send me two platy . . ." And there he stops. Platy-*what?* Here it is, a minute to five on Friday afternoon, everyone in the zoo office has gone home, his program doesn't have a spell-check for exotic animal names, and he doesn't know the plural of *platypus.* Is it *platypuses?* No, that sounds too silly; it can't be right. *Platypi?* That sounds worse. So what's he going to do? The e-mail has to go out. And so he sends it, requesting two of what he wants. Can you guess how he does it?

Easy, easy as pie. Just watch how and learn. He backs up to his letter's salutation, taps it in once again to establish his rhythm, and fires away. "Dear National Zoo of Australia," he writes, "please send me one platypus!" Here I'd pause for effect, then continue in a less emphatic tone: "And, while you're at it, why don'tcha send me another one, too?"

There would be as many groans as laughs, but by now everyone knew this was part of the plan: what was funny about these jokes was that they were *bad* jokes, tired old howlers from my own childhood so many years before. But an educational point was being made nonetheless, and not about how to fudge your way through uncertain plurals. Why is any such joke funny? One of America's best comic writers, Kurt Vonnegut, has explained why. The first part is a question, here an implied question: what is the proper plural form of *platypus?* Agreed, that's a tough one. But in essence, all questions are tough, because they ask us to think, and think-

ing is damned hard work. In Vonnegut's own favorite joke, the question is explicit: Why does cream cost so much? His answer is genuinely hilarious: Because the cows really hate squatting over those tiny little bottles. But why does it make people laugh? Because, after being asked to think (hard work!), they are acquitted of the responsibility (relief!), and hence the happy laughter comes. After the emotional test of Grace Paley's "Samuel," it's time for a laugh, and sometimes even Grace will build them into her stories. There are some instances of that in the first story we'd talk about next Monday, "The Burdened Man," so note how her use of language—specifically, the story's tone of voice—contributes to what otherwise would be matters of plot and theme. But just as a reminder that Grace can be deadly serious about language, too (as all poets must be from time to time), read "The Little Girl" as well, keeping an eye on (or rather an ear open to) this same question. And watch out, there would be some very disturbing things in "The Little Girl."

Having interfaced Dixon and Paley, contrasts between a heavily narrative and more vocally poetic approach could be appreciated. That's the joy of a course like Introduction to Literature. You can have it both ways: reading an author in some depth, with time to see a fictive methodology evolve, but then also being able to contrast it (in equal depth) with the entirely different way another author might write. To me, this seemed so much more effective than the combined anthology and genre approaches, where a bunch of single stories by various authors are knocked off one at a time before switching so unrelatedly to an equal number of poems and poets. In our day especially, genre has ceased to be a major concern, replaced by a fascination with writing as activity. Not to say that fiction, poetry, and drama don't have distinctions, just that the distinctions are now more likely to be employed within one piece. In a story such as "The Burdened Man," Grace does it effortlessly (both for herself and for her readers). And the easiest way into it is by thinking about voice (for Paley) rather than about character and its resultant plot complications (as had been done successfully for Dixon).

"The man has the burden of the money," we're told in the first line in page 109. But what's the burden: horrendous payments, catastrophic expenses, a life-and-death struggle to survive? Not at all. Here, for once, Grace gives us some details, and look how ridiculous his worries are: over pennies wasted on electricity or lost in spare change. And when he comes to blows with the neighbor lady over such a paltry amount, such a fight that the police are called, why aren't they arrested? Again, because of some cu-

riously noted details: the fact that they live on a street with shady trees and neatly kept lawns. Is it odd that in the aftermath they contemplate (but do not consummate) an affair? Maybe so, but look at the strange way Grace phrases their intimacy: "They each tell one story about when they were young" (111). That, friends, can be every bit as intimate as sex, surely more intimate than casual sex. So maybe the lady's husband is justified after all when he confronts their supposed adultery.

The language in this story is the obvious clue to the meaning of its action, and the most violent scene—when the husband, a drunkenly enraged police officer, does a complete shoot-'em-up—is rendered not only sparely but in precisely chosen words. The cop doesn't aim and fire his weapon but "waved it before his eyes as though it could clear fogs and smogs" (113–14). No gun can do that, but a crazy drunk might think so—and look how nicely Grace's language makes that point. The wife enrages him further by citing an embarrassment from his professional past; such is the power of uxorial intimacy, she knows exactly how to hurt him. As for him hurting her, did you notice Grace's care with the shot pattern? Right: all over. Can you tell the size gun he's using? Is it his service-issue .38? No, it's something big and unstable, most likely a clip-loaded .45. Cops carry them, but as their own personal weapon. Why? Because if a gorilla is coming at you with a weapon of his own, a bullet from a .38, even straight through the heart, is not going to stop him. But a hit from a .45 almost anywhere on the torso will, not only halting his momentum but blowing him backwards, just like you see in the movies and on TV. Did Grace learn this from watching TV? Perhaps. But as will be explained in a few minutes, Grace has been around and is pretty damned tough.

Her burdened man of this story winds up softened, though, doesn't he? He survives his shoulder wound, moves to another neighborhood, and "until old stage startled him, he was hardly unhappy again" (115). He is "hardly unhappy" for a very simple reason: he's faced death and come through it, an experience that puts the nickels and dimes of this world in perspective. It's a pretty simple story, when you think about it; in terms of having a message, it's just a cliché. But Grace Paley is no writer of clichés. Instead, she's taken a situation we thought we all knew about and recast it in exceptional language that makes us see and think as we may not have before.

Okay, you want to know how Grace knows so much about police firepower? Yes, she's from New York, where if the newscasts listed all the murders each day, they'd have to run all day without making a repeat, right? She's also been involved in social protests, has been arrested, and has even

served some time in jail. But to look at her, she looks like Grandma. Born in 1922, half a generation older than Steve. Father a doctor, but not a rich one—self-made immigrant, worked his way up from the bottom, and so on. If that sounds like a cliché, flip to page 122 in the volume's title story for a description: "He remembered the first time he'd seen the American flag on wild Ellis Island. Under its protection and working like a horse, he'd read Dickens, gone to medical school, and shot like a surface-to-air missile right into the middle class." As a doctor's daughter and a bright one to boot, Grace had been able to go to college. Not every woman did back then, but Grace started at Hunter College, finishing up at secretarial school when she got married. By the time she started writing, she had kids and was looking at divorce—that's why she's written so few stories, just three or four dozen compared to Steve's five hundred-some. But as a divorced mother with two kids in New York City, she learned to be tough.

The toughness is evident in "The Little Girl," isn't it? If you look at the author's photo and think she resembles your grandmother, fine; but why would Grandma write a story like this? A fourteen-year-old runaway is raped, beaten, and murdered—awful enough, but Grace makes it even worse by giving a graphic description of the assault's physical aftermath. Almost like an autopsy, the details are revolting in their simple clinical precision. Why on earth does she do this? There's no suspense whatsoever about the occasion; you know exactly what's going to happen, given who the girl is, who the guys are. The girl's an innocent, even naive little thing from the Middle West; the guys are . . . yes, the guys are New York City ghetto blacks. How do you know that? I mean, how early in the story can you tell that the narrator is an African American living in a depressed part of the inner city? Right: second word of the first sentence, "Carter stop by the café early" (152). Not *stops,* not *stopped.* Second sentence confirms it: "I just done waxing." You know the term for it: *Ebonics,* the linguistic style of black people in the city, at least of some black people in some cities. But what society has generalized from it is how black ghetto folks speak on TV.

So is Grace dealing in stereotypes? She has indeed used stereotypical speech right off, but do all the African Americans in her story speak this way? Not at all, because when her narrator proceeds to quote his friend Carter (in just the third and fourth sentences, plenty early for first impressions), the black speech is a little different: "He said, I believe I'm having company later on." Smooth, slick; correct grammar but intimidating nonetheless, perhaps even more so because of the studied correctness: "Let me use your place, Charlie, hear?"

Again, we know the type: this is how pimps talk, or at least how they talk on TV. But rather than just type-casting her characters, Grace is asking us to hear how they speak, because the point of what happens in this story is their verbal manner and what comes of it. Look ahead to page 153 and see how smoothly Carter sweet-talks the little girl, telling her just what she wants to hear after fleeing her overdirective parents and living on the run for who knows how many days, tired and dirty, hungry and uncertain: "He says, I got a nice place you could just relax and rest and decide what to do next. Take a shower. My, my you are sweet. You better'n Miss America. How old did you say you was?"

Eighteen? No way. To suspect she's really in her very early teens, all we have to do is listen to her speak—or, more properly, hear how Charlie, our narrator, renders her speech. It's total immaturity, all teenage babble with irrational non sequiturs. Don't you have a little sister at home, thirteen or fourteen, who views the world like this, with unreasonable parents, troublesome siblings, and all? Charlie's got her down perfectly, just as he's captured the essence of Carter's seductive lilt. It's all in the language.

And then the little girl is assaulted, raped, and murdered, torn savagely and thrown from a high window. We're told all this in plain, almost clinical language, almost like a coroner's report. Well, it's believable that Charlie is familiar with this style of language, too, given the violent world he lives in. But look what happens next: Charlie goes through the scene all over again. Wasn't once was enough?

No, considering the difference this second time around, a difference signaled by the narrator's language. This time, he's not standing in for the coroner but instead taking it from another point of view: the little girl's. Talk about a breakthrough. Here he is, imagining the crime from the victim's point of view, identifying with her suffering. Read the passage carefully, and see his empathy. And don't ever think Grace Paley would say all men are jerks. Some are, but not this case, where Grace accords her male character with opportunities of insight and change. Only by such strategies can we hope for all the brutalities such as have been described to end.

But—at least one student would always make a good objection: wasn't Charlie just rationalizing the event, particularly when he imagines the little girl being so devastated that she throws herself out the window, thereby absolving Charlie's friends of murder?

Well, I'd offer, that's a possibility. Particularly if the story ended right there. What's the last thing Charlie says? "That what I think right now" (158).

But is that the story's last line? No, after a paragraph break, one short

sentence follows: "That is what happened." Is this Charlie's language, the Ebonics in which everything preceding has been accounted? No, it is proper, standard speech, the way Grace Paley herself would say it. And because of the noticeable shift in grammar, we have to suspect she's making that point, saying Charlie has imagined it correctly. Take his creator's word for it: he's got it right.

With three of her stories covered, it would be time for some personal notes. The best story to tell about Grace was my friend Jerry Rosen's, about how she was the only writer he'd ever met who could give a formal reading while chewing gum. I'd demonstrate the difference, reading the first lines of "Samuel" the way a conventional poet or fiction writer might present it in a formal setting during a campus visit and then how Grace Paley's speaking manner conveys the material, gum lodged in one side of her mouth and words being barked out of the other, pure New York car driver. I'd pass around some photos of Grace, the well-known ones where she's outfitted for social activism. How does this grandma dress? Look at her: longshoreman' wool hat, sweatshirt, parka, jeans, tennis shoes. All that sends a message just as clear as her speech: tough and practical. Did I know her? Yes, but just a phone friendship and one that was always being interrupted by her second husband, just recently married when I started work on her back in the seventies: Robert Nichols, a retired ad man who wanted to become a writer and kept pushing his books at me for review. Were his books any good? Not really, and that made things awkward. I'd show some photos of him and make catty little remarks, good for a joke. Was I jealous? Only intellectually. But that's the deepest channel in which jealousy runs.

Grace's activism would make a good preparation for the stories up for next class, "The Long Distance Runner" and "A Conversation with My Father," two more examples of how qualities of voice motivate the action. What were her issues? Nothing offensive (this is rural Iowa, remember), just the typical things a divorced mother with two kids might logically be concerned with. Yes, she had protested the war in Vietnam, but more for maternal than political reasons. In the war's aftermath, she had published her most famous protest statement, "Other People's Children," in the September 1975 issue of *Ms.* magazine. Her complaint was about the massive babylift effort preceding the fall of Saigon, when so many orphans were brought to safety with adoptive parents in the United States. What was wrong with doing that, students would ask—isn't it maternal to want these kids to have fathers and mothers? Well, that's Grace's point: these babies

already had mothers, mothers who were surely looking for them at the time. Yes, the carnage of war had separated them, but here was a misconstrued aid effort that made their separation permanent. Imagine the despair of a mother looking so frantically for her baby and finding that it had been shipped off to the U.S.A. Only men could have conceived such a program, Grace told her readers. Think about it—she's probably right.

She'd done jail time for her protests. Nothing violent: at the worst blocking a street, at its messiest pouring blood on the lawn at the White House. In New York, she'd been held several days at the Women's House of Detention, the place where the small-time drug dealers and prostitutes go. They were deeply offended that Grace was thrown in among them and protested on her behalf. What did they say? Well, I'll have to use the F word, okay? Okay. They raised a ruckus, shouting, "Get this fucking housewife outta here!" See, sisterhood is powerful.

There's a sisterhood of sorts that develops in "The Long Distance Runner," but Grace is careful to present it as a shared motherhood. Wait a minute, students would ask, what kind of mother would run out on her kids for three weeks, just leaving them for the neighbor lady to look in on? Give me a minute, I'd plead—I can explain that. But consider this first: can't you think of a point in time when your own mother might have *liked* to take off like that? And don't you think it could have been good for her if she did? Your parents are about the narrator's age, late forties. The story doesn't use this term, but what's the pop psychology label for what the woman is undergoing? *Midlife crisis.* "The Long Distance Runner" is one example of how such thinking gains currency, after all. *Psychology Today* and Gail Sheehy didn't invent the experience; people did, and as people like Grace Paley began writing about it back in the sixties and early seventies, psychologists took note. Just wait 'til we get to Michael Stephens and Alice Walker, when you'll see some other experiences and attitudes toward them that you may have thought existed for all time but that actually show genesis in their works—*this is how culture happens.*

Also sports. Yes, indeed, you can see the genesis of a certain style of exercise activity in this story. To fight off middle-age sag, the woman has taken up running, an aerobic strategy just coming into vogue when this piece was written. But running's not there to be trendy. Look how nicely it fits the narrator's situation, so much better than getting out the stair-step and popping in a video of *Buns of Steel*. Long-distance running gets her out of the house and, what is even more important, out of the mental confines that have been boxing her in and into the free-flowing world of the

runner's high. You all know about that, and its sense of liberation provides the credibility for her running as far as her old neighborhood in Brooklyn. Once there, coming to earth in what is now a dangerous ghetto, she's able to sustain it by finding a point of sympathy with the otherwise hostile people and moving in—to her family's old apartment!—for three weeks.

What does Grace Paley's narrator do in the old apartment, now occupied by a black woman and her children? She does something along the same lines as the runner's high, something women seem able to do so easily, suspending time and space and other distractions in favor of one simply gratifying activity: talking. Yakking, if you want to put it that way. But either way, it works, and by the end, our middle-aged woman has come out of her midlife crisis. How does she do it? Returning home (where she hasn't even been missed), she tells her teenaged kids and her boyfriend where she's been and what she's done. "What?" they ask—go ahead, pronounce it as such guys would: "Whaaa?" So she retells them (and us) the story in just a few words, making its point crystal clear:

> Because it isn't usually so simple. Have you known it to happen much nowadays? A woman inside the steamy energy of middle age runs and runs. She finds the houses and streets where her childhood happened. She lives in them. She learns as though she was still a child what in the world is coming next. (198)

Here I could get into what everybody liked best: telling the students about life. A good idea, for what else are works of literature about, why else are they written? And why should we read them, other than to see how with artful effect they make their point. What's so important about worrying about what comes next? Simple: until well into middle age, you never have to worry about that. The future has always been taken care of, from your next diaper change and feeding to your class schedule, marriage, and job responsibilities, and so forth. But by age fifty all that's taken care of—kids raised, your business running itself, and so forth. All of a sudden, for the first time in your life, you don't really know what's coming next. Listen to me, it's a truly eerie emptiness you can feel, like a cartoon character running off the edge of the cliff and then looking down. It is what Grace's character has been feeling, and look how she resolves the fear: by going back to her childhood home, where next steps were always taken care of by others, and reorients herself to family life.

Talking things over carries on as the narrative motivator in the last Grace Paley story we'd read, "A Conversation with My Father." Here would be a

situation students could more easily understand, of making a nursing home visit to an aged relative. What's the major ground rule for such occasions? Right, don't rile the old folks up. Say yes to everything, no matter how befuddled they seem. Here the situation is even more delicate, as the narrator's father wants to lecture her about the techniques of story writing, specifically the moral closure of endings. She's a short story writer, just like Grace. He's a retired doctor, just as was Grace's father, a Russian-Jewish immigrant from the old school who favors nineteenth-century masters such as Maupassant and Chekhov. Does Grace's character write tales like theirs? Not at all, as a quoted example shows—if anything, her stories are even stranger than Paley's, though the affinities are clear. The father demands a resolution; her daughter resists, not wanting to sentence her characters to anything other than "the open destiny of life" (162). "How long will it be?" he challenges her at the story's end. "Tragedy! You too. When will you look it in the face?" (167). Any idea what he means and why his daughter resists it?

Taught to look for special language, the students would note how the father's health is first described: not good, with "his heart, that bloody motor" close to failing (161). *That bloody motor*—handwriting on the wall? A gun hanging on the wall, waiting to be fired, now that its odd presence has been noted? But who's resisting closure? The daughter herself, about the impending loss of her own father. And that's the final lesson he's striving to teach her.

Any extra punch to this lesson? Of course. Look on page 3, at the author's disclaimer, a necessary piece of business customarily stating that all of the persons, places, and events in the following stories were fictitious, any correspondences to actual persons, places, and events being coincidental. You say that, quite rightly, so you don't get sued. But Grace's disclaimer is styled differently, using language more poetically and also breaking one of fiction's first rules: "Everyone in this book is imagined into life except the father. No matter what story he has to live in, he's my father, I. Goodside, M.D., artist, and storyteller. G. P." Think about it: if the elderly man in "A Conversation with My Father" is Grace Paley's real-life parent, isn't Grace herself the daughter? The story-in-a-story her narrator writes is certainly Paleyesque, and the critical arguments she makes are quite pertinent to Grace Paley's style of writing. It's an interesting way to fold both the textures of life and of fiction into a short story, a strategy that gives added authority to what she writes.

So there: you've learned a lot about Grace Paley, by herself and in com-

parison with Steve Dixon. Steve and Grace are friends, by the way; she taught for a semester as a visiting prof at Johns Hopkins, and they admire each other's work. In fact, Steve has his own "conversation with my father story," which can be summarized quickly. It's called "Time to Go" and appears in Steve's collection with that same title; it came out ten years after Grace's book and can be taken as a response. And it's a good one. Just listen.

A man is out shopping for an engagement present to give his fiancée. His father is along, which seems odd, but to make it worse, the old man gives an endless stream of advice, butting into impending sales to warn that the son is being a spendthrift, that there are better ways to approach the clerk and better bargains to be had across the street. That's the first part, of three. In the second part, the man and his fiancée are together, picking out wedding rings—and there's the father again, counseling deals and trying to guide the son's choice. Lord, we think, it must have been gauche enough having the father embarrass his son with the salespeople first time, but now in front of the young woman herself . . . And then we notice: the clerks don't seem to hear the hectoring, nor does the fiancée. Aaaaaahhhhhh, we realize: the father's not there in person, just in the son's conscience. Isn't that true for you? Listen, to this day, I can't reach for a wrong tool without hearing my father say, "Jerome! You'll botch it! Take a minute and go find the right screwdriver . . ." That's what parents are for, right? So it's a nice little story. All that instruction stays with you. But this is only the second part. There's a third section, where the man, now a happy groom, is celebrating with family and friends at the wedding reception. All has been perfect, except for one thing: where's Dad? Searching the room, the son finds him, sitting alone off in a corner and crying. The son rushes to him, asks why the tears, and is told, "Because I am so happy for you." The father rises, embraces his son, and disappears.

As a response to Grace's story, it works—as a Steve Dixon story. Narrative finesse rather than poetic language, tricky action instead of modulations of voice—these are reminders of how differently Steve approaches an otherwise similar subject. Two writers, down, two to go, with comparisons and contrasts already adding up. Time for a break, okay? At approximately the halfway point of this double-time, half-semester course, and with an unpopular Friday meeting date approaching, I'd give the students a day off. You've been wanting to get out of here early the last two weeks, I know; people have jobs, people have business at home that needs tending, people have activities. So here's your chance: no class, no joke. But

take advantage of the break to do some thinking about Grace and Steve, thinking about them together. And as the next book would be a novel, start reading it now. *Season at Coole* by Michael Stephens is an extended narrative generated by considerations of family, both in theme and in structure. So as you read the first chapter, take note of what the family structure is and how certain things make it ripe for disruption. That's the question for Monday. Read on if you can, and note the contrasts between chapter 2 and chapter 3: one's about the eldest son in the family, Leland Jr.; the other's about one of the daughters, Oona. Consider how the way each chapter is written corresponds to how different the two siblings are. If you really get on a roll, next Friday (and there will be a joke, the Famous Stalactite/Stalagmite Joke) we'll talk about chapters 4 (on Emmett—does crime pay?) and 5 (on Sandra, nicknamed Sam—does sex pay?). That's how we'll proceed through the book, examining the siblings and judging their ways out of the family.

Following our improvised midsemester break a curiously energized class would return with one big question about *Season at Coole*. Most had taken my advice and spent some time sorting out Dixon and Paley, building up critical confidence, and plunging into Michael Stephens. They didn't know yet that Michael had lived a childhood in conditions similar to those described in the novel. Nor had I told them that Michael was scarcely twenty years old when he'd written this book, about their age or younger. But the family's doings were such wild stuff that I wouldn't even have to ask the question about all the possibilities for disruption. The students would start class by asking me: Is this family dysfunctional?

Something else happened that first semester and recurred almost every time I've taught the novel since. After a couple sessions, where we'd dealt with the parents and the older siblings (in their substance abuse and moments of madness) and gotten into the middle gang of kids (and their experiments with sex and art), a previously quiet student would linger after class, waiting until everyone else left, and approach me with the confession that his or her own family was much like this one—especially after I'd revealed some of the autobiographical details. Michael himself, along with Steve Dixon one of my closest literary friends, would ponder these admissions over the years. It didn't surprise him that more and more students were talking about dysfunction and so readily using the word; there was more and more dysfunction out there every year. What impressed these previously silent people was that someone else shared the experience *and*

had written about it—written about it to share the experience, yes, but also to make from it a work of art. Perhaps it took chapter 6, Patrick and Michael's chapter (for which I'd ask, "Does art pay?"), better yet, chapter 7 (devoted to the mother and with the simple question in mind, "Does Michael love his mother?") to elicit these responses. Then, in the last two chapters, one could find hope, both in the way the three youngest siblings plan better lives for themselves and in the way the crisis that begins the book is resolved.

That's a pretty grand sweep and would mark the difference between the short stories we'd been reading and the novel at hand. But there were other elements in Michael's work we'd be attending to from the start, notably his lyrical use of language and his dramatic use of events. These were different from Paley's verbal nuances and Dixon's narrative actions; when it came to words, Michael Stephens was a singer, and as for choreographed behavior, his characters were histrionic to the point of being actors, and he himself so in tune with them as to be the dramatist of their fates. Points like these emerged slowly, with the same caution shown by the children of dysfunction with their secret confessions. Five class periods would be devoted to Michael's work, as many as to Alice Walker's stories (handled at a deliberate pace for enjoyment of their sentimentality) when we'd end the course. But with a workshop of techniques learned from Dixon and Paley, it was time now for an extended experience with literature—a whole family, a whole segment of life, a whole novel. It wouldn't be the easiest week and a half for reading or for thinking, but from the start it seemed worth the effort.

Starting off the course with *Season at Coole* could have been a disaster. But after just seven intensive class meetings devoted to handling Steve's and Grace's stories, meeting the authors on a first-name basis and working with their material in a strongly personal way, the most naive students could now be confident with Michael's otherwise daunting work. The language wouldn't be any more poetic than they'd seen in Paley, the action any more bizarre than in Dixon's most extreme demonstrations; but the length of it, the amount of time they were immersed in this extended literary experience, would be something that impressed students—impressed them *with themselves,* with their ability to digest a work so close to the otherwise unspeakable aspects of their own lives or the life of a friend. The father, the mother, or any one of the nine children could have made nice character sketches or excuses for an inventive plot exercise. But here they

were all together in a full-length novel, just as they were jammed together in the Coole household on the tension-building night before Christmas, where the seasonal demands for functionality make the family's sorry condition all the worse. Even if their families were perfect, students could still appreciate how the big three holidays (Thanksgiving, Christmas, New Year's) coming so close together create a burden of both expectations and responsibilities. *There's* the potential for disruption, all right. And to think that this major work was written by someone no older than themselves, who—as I'd tell them in the course of this Monday class—graduated from high school and had to decide whether to become a writer or become a hoodlum like some of his brothers . . . *Season at Coole* hit home.

Details of disruptiveness abound throughout the first chapter, and the class would enjoy listing them. The father's beer intake and resultant alcoholic rages; the mother's escape into the sweet dreams of cheap wine; the children's use of marijuana, hashish, amphetamines, and other controlled substances: these were hardly foundations for family stability. And look how they behaved; look at the conditions in which they lived, with motorcycle parts stored in the kitchen, dishes kept out in the garage (to discourage use and the need to wash them), and so forth. But there's a disruption in the language, too, a dramatic dance of mixed metaphors and disjunctive similes that makes for a particularly mad song. We see it right from the start, not just in the father's mad mosaic of paternal curses but also in the supposedly reliable, third-person omniscience that describes the scene, where trouble is mounting because Leland Coole and Leland Coole Jr. "had decided to go off the edge of the planet like a brace of ducks in orange sauce together, a duet for father and son" (12). Here, less than five hundred words into the narrative, we're asked to visualize the impossible: ducks flying not across the sky but into space, and cooked in orange sauce as well. It gets worse (and thus in literary terms better), when the father hears the phone ring, is annoyed that it's probably another of the million calls his teenage daughter has been getting, and lunges for the offending instrument:

> The old man was running to grab the phone out of his daughter's hand, he plowed through the room like a hippo after a nature photographer, a wild boar stalking meat, Black Irish Coole was grabbing the phone out of his daughter's hand, the receiver went dead, his black eyes like a predatory bird, his long

beaked nose, the curly black hair, except for the bald spot in
the back, his body was a pear, and rising up and down from
the excursion, like a bellows, the belly hanging over the belt of
his pants, the cuffs dragging along the floor, hobbling from one
foot to the other to keep the weight off the ingrown toenail on
his right foot, and then keeping the weight off the ingrown
toenail on his left foot, he tripped over his cuffs and was en-
tangled in the phone wire, frantically trying to extract himself
from this condition. (19)

An encyclopedia of poetic techniques can be compiled from just this
portion of a paragraph, but two more features are important: how the comparisons are so multiform and rhythmically incantatory that they take on
a life of their own (the song), and how the subject of this lyric language is
danced through it all into an exquisitely timed pratfall (the drama). The
lesson is obvious, as once again an author has taught us how to read his
work within the first few pages. Drama and song will shape each experience, be it in life or in the text.

One thing that really helped my students move into the greater expanses
of a novel was Michael's sense of structure. From chapters 1 through 9 he
works his way through the family and from room to room in the house
where the various members live, from the eldest son in the basement (where
his schizophrenic lifestyle fits the cesspool atmosphere) to the youngest
siblings in the attic, where childhood hopes still soar high. Leland Jr. is
mad, and his language shows it, tumbling off the page in manic hysteria.
Meanwhile, his sister Oona, small and quiet, wafts herself away on pot and
hashish, in a quieter chapter that, like herself, is a fraction of the size of
Leland (and his own gross section of the novel). After all the introductory
mayhem, students could appreciate the contrast, especially the young
woman's silences, in which "words evaporated around her" (59). Isn't that
nicely put, after all the noise in Leland Jr.'s chapter, all those rants and raves
threatening to spill off the page? But notice how neither of these siblings'
ways are effective ways out; Leland Jr. is consumed by self-hatred, while
Oona resides in self-absorption.

In preparation for Friday's class (and the Famous Stalactite/Stalagmite
Joke), I'd offer some facts about Michael. Three years younger than me,
his punkish ways always made him seem even more junior; when we met,
back in the early seventies when *Season at Coole* was just out and recom-

mended to me by Michael's editor, I was trying to act a lot older than I was, whereas my new friend seemed dedicated to remaining immature. That's a harsh word, I know, but in my studied probity, that's how he impressed me. How was he immature? Well, picture this: here I come into New York from Iowa, a geographical leap that's contrast enough, but on top of it, I'm journeying from a nice brick house in a shaded neighborhood with a wife and two little kids into the mean streets of lower New York City, to a factory district just now becoming an area for artists' lofts, a place called "SoHo" (for "south of Houston," pronounced "HOW-ston," a major east-west thoroughfare). Rents were still cheap, which is why Michael was there. But he didn't even have his own place. Instead, his letter had directed me to an address near Spring and Greene Streets, where I was to climb five steep flights to a sculptor's studio where Michael was borrowing some living space.

And what kind of space was it—a spare bedroom, or perhaps a sofa bed? Nope. I'd describe what a loft is like, with all its open space and improvised living areas, and give the class a feeling for the light manufacturing that had gone on here years ago and the noise a metal sculptor would be making now, and then express how surprised I was at where Michael was "living": in a corner of this huge room where he'd spread a pallet on the floor next to some books and a clock radio. Holy hell, our cat had better quarters back home on Clay Street! To have a decent conversation, we had to leave the noisy loft and find a quiet booth in a bar and grill around the corner. Here we ate lunch, drank beer, and talked for several hours, tape recording an interview on Michael's work. Yes, *Season at Coole* had some correspondences with his life; his family wasn't exactly like this, but they had their moments, enough of them to convince Michael he never wanted to start one of his own. I'll never forget the way he phrased it, which despite the many beers we shared was pretty sobering. "It's one of the great tragedies of life," he explained, polishing off the German import I'd paid for and looking around for the waiter to summon another, "that every human being is cursed with having had to have a mother and having had to have a father."

For crying out loud, I had a mother and father and loved them, just as I knew my own children loved me and their own mother now. This was a terrible attitude to have, sad and also chilling. I found it hard to talk about the theme of family life after that, but Michael had made himself clear. His pallet on the factory floor was a statement, a counter-statement to my

own Lay-Z-Boy recliner and king-sized bed and everything else back in Cedar Falls. But it's his life, I figured, and in his free choice of how to live it, he'd crafted a beautiful novel, a terrible beauty as William Butler Yeats so famously put it. Yeats, James Joyce, Flann O'Brien—these were Michael's saints, the Irish guides to his profoundly Irish-American style of writing.

Back at the loft, it was quieter, all the metal sculpting done for the day, and Michael suggested I stay a bit and meet his girlfriend. Once she arrived, I knew why: he wanted me to see what a gorgeous knockout she was, a soap opera actress fresh from the TV studio uptown. This became the pattern of my subsequent visits: Michael would always be at another borrowed address, sometimes sleeping on a friend's couch, other times back on the floor, and always with an heiress or some such, but always someone different. Three months seemed to be as long as he'd let a relationship continue. He did *not* want anything lasting or serious, and in my tape recorder I had the reason why.

Imagine my surprise, then, when after a couple years of this, he phoned to say he was getting married. Married? Michael Stephens? So which actress or model was it? "She's not an actress; she's a singer," he explained. "A night club singer? A pop star?" I wanted to know. No, she was a student of classical voice studying at Julliard, and when I came to New York next I could meet her. When I did, I was surprised at who she was: not some Iowa fantasy of a Radio City Music Hall Rockette but a quiet young woman named Ok-Hee Yu, who'd left Seoul, Korea, to complete her education and begin teaching voice in Manhattan. Did Michael have any idea of what he was doing? Yes he did, as the marriage lasted, and they had a bright and beautiful daughter, Moira Me-Ok, and the once-punkish Michael Stephens swore off alcohol (writing a book about it, *Green Dreams*) and learning how Ok-Hee's Korean family was marvelously functional, over there on the other side of the earth where Michael could write a book about that as well: *Lost in Seoul,* which is very much *Season at Coole* inside out and upside down.

Yet even as a good husband and loving father, my friend Michael has plenty of the street punk in him, I'd explain, while preparing the students for chapter 4 on brother Emmett (and his life of crime) and chapter 5 on sister Sandra (and her life of sex). He's had plenty of good teaching jobs at some glorious places: Columbia, Princeton, even the flagship of Jesuit schools, Fordham University, to which my brightest friends at Marquette High won scholarships. But he's always walked away from them, often with some chip on his shoulder. One place, where he'd had an endowed chair

and seemed set for life, had to be scuttled because—honest to God!—Michael told me people were looking at him funny. But he's not a bum. When he leaves one job, he replaces it with another, often with more effort required. What he prizes is his independence. Perhaps that's how he talked himself out of the mother-father curse that he'd made me feel so badly the day we met.

Friday's class on Emmett and Sandra would have a strong Irish flavor to it. I'm half Irish, McNamara on my mother's side, so I could ham up the ethnicity. Emmett himself is enough of a cartoon character (pure Bart Simpson, later classes would say) that his chapter is appealingly funny, despite the fact that he lives by crime—victimless crime, sometimes abetted by the police. Plus, he's compulsively neat, a contrast to Leland Jr.'s gross excesses. His presence generates comedy of the adorably slapstick manner made so appealing by Laurel and Hardy. Michael Stephens describes the scene of his latest arrest with wonderfully paced mayhem, bringing in (as the students could already indicate) the father's boozy wrath, the mother's woozy sentimentality, Leland Jr.'s schizoid rage, the younger children's clamor ("gathered around the police like a slew of Oliver Twists, poor and depraved looking like a Dickens dream of squalor," as we're told on page 74), even the baby squalling in its crib. But from Emmett, we move on to Sandra, caught up in the blooming of sexuality. There are even hints of incest. Are you shocked? No, students would reply—she and her brother don't actually do it; they just talk about it. Does talking help? It seems to—at the very least, it keeps them from trying it. Okay, so there's a clue: we read on, see who else steps aside from the action to talk, to put things into words rather than actions, into art rather than life.

Looking back on the scenes we'd discussed in detail—the old man's rage with the telephone, the son's arrest amid the family's wildness, "an Ivesian symphony of dissonance and American transcendental yatter" (76), as we were told—students could see the physical evidence contributing to aesthetic effect. The action might be wild, but the words for it were wilder. Perhaps it should be the words that got our major attention? And not just for their art, but for what such art could do for otherwise nasty life?

Now for Friday's customary reward, another joke from my ancient childhood. You've toured caves, right? There are the stalactites hanging down like icicles, the stalagmites growing up like daggers thrust from the floor, striving to reach the cave's roof. Okay—how do you remember which is which? Easy: a stalactite holds on to the roof as tight as it can, while a stalagmite, if it keeps growing up someday might reach the top and become

a stalactite. Right, that's more of a mnemonic device than a joke, but I thought it was pretty funny when I heard it as a kid up in Cave of the Mounds near Madison. But here's something funny. A couple years ago my wife and I were in Ireland and stopped to tour a cave, where I wondered if the guide would tell the same story. Did he? No, he didn't, and I was disappointed. What he did was take us all the way in, turn out the lights to show us how pitch black it was, then light a match and tell us how the cave was discovered.

"Well, da farmer was out with da dog, huntin' da rabbit," he said (this was in Ireland, remember, so I'd have to do the accent). "An da rabbit runs in the bush an disappears. Da dog goes in da bush after da rabbit an da dog disappears. So da farmer looks into da bush an lo an behold dere's da entrance to da cave!"

Pretty lame story, right? Well, the guide went on telling how the farmer reached in his pocket for a candle (he's out hunting rabbits with a candle?), lights it with the only match he has (hey, wait: if he's gone to the trouble of carrying a candle, why doesn't he have a full book?), and with the risk of being lost forever if his candle blows out continues on several thousand feet into this dark-as-midnight cave. Here we are today, then, enjoying the farmer's grand discovery.

"An will dere be any questions?" the guide asked. You bet I had a question! At this point, I'd explain how as I raised my hand to ask, my wife moved away from me and stood next to another guy. She's seen me in situations like this many times and hates to be embarrassed.

"Ah, da gentleman with da beard: an what is your question, sar?"

Pretty obvious, I implied, asking, "Did the dog get the rabbit?"

Well, wasn't that the whole point of the guide's story? Sorry, but the Cave of the Mounds story was better, don't you think? At least there's something to learn, and this is general education, where you've got to learn *everything* before graduation.

Chapter 6, on Patrick (the painter) and Michael (the writer), would be up for Monday's class, together with chapter 7, given over to the mother. Chapter 7's sweet, I'd advise. Of course, Michael loves his mother—every Irish son loves his mother, no matter what he says to a critic after sucking up a few (or more than a few) beers. But be prepared for some nastiness in the second half of chapter 6. If it disgusts you, skip it—you'll know what Michael's getting at. It has to do with art and the fact that beyond whether or not art pays, art is not necessarily easy. In the novel, Patrick paints en-

ergetic, even violent canvases, while Michael Coole writes energetic, even violent descriptions.

Hence, Monday's class would be more serious, rightly so as chapters 6 and 7 are the points at which the novel begins turning toward its resolution. As in Grace Paley's "The Long Distance Runner," talking things over helps, as Patrick and Michael rehearse their family's idiocies in a way that makes the storytelling of it almost worth the suffering. But verbal embellishment can take on its own nastiness, too, which is why the novel gives us a scene where the boys' aunt goes nuts at a hockey game. Balancing it out is chapter 7, where the mother is presented in an affectionate, nonjudgmental way: a little girl playing hookey from her family.

Grace Paley had resisted closure, feeling that resolutions boxed in her characters. But in Michael Stephens's novel, the characters are seeking to get out. Does the ending help them do this? The three youngest still have their hopes, and in self-discipline, sports, and childlike love, each sees more promise than do the older siblings. Yet for an all-encompassing resolution, we must look to the mother, who accomplishes it by a brilliantly successful strategy: taking away her husband's excuses.

Why is this so effective? Think about it: if you're trying to get someone off alcohol, for example (one of Leland Sr.'s vices), have you succeeded if you simply take away the booze? No—he or she can always find an excuse to go back and get some more. But when you've taken away a person's *excuses* for abuse, you've pointed him or her toward recovery. It was a technique Michael, who has written about his own problems in *Green Dreams,* used in his own life, after mastering it in fiction.

Was Michael Stephens still sober? Yes. Was he still a punk? Yes, but appealingly so: he was working on being the world's oldest, most reliable, most self-disciplined punk. Editing *Writing Baseball,* I could give classes an example how. Here I was, I'd explain, with the director of the University of Illinois Press asking me to assemble a collection of baseball writing, fictive and nonfictive prose, to accompany an already-acquired volume of baseball poems. Looking around, I found lots of material to reprint but wanted some new stuff, too. I asked my friend Jerry Rosen to write up the story he'd told me of how as a teenager he'd been a guest batboy for the old New York Giants and, while shagging batting practice, had inadvertently called off Willie Mays. I asked my friend Rick Wolff to write up the story he'd told me about how, as a middle-aged New York editor, he'd returned to play a real game at shortstop for a real team in the same Class A

minor league where he'd had a brief career twenty years before. And of course, I phoned Michael Stephens to ask if he had anything on baseball I'd overlooked.

"Naah," Michael dismissed my inquiry, "I don't have anything on baseball. Don't you want something on boxing? I have plenty of stuff on boxing; Joyce Carol Oates used one of my boxing pieces in her book."

"No, Michael," I tried to explain, "this isn't an anthology for all sports, it's just for baseball. Don't you have *anything?*"

"Naah," he repeated, anxious to end this part of the conversation and get on to telling me about his book on Korea.

"But Michael," I insisted, "I have a budget from the Press. I can pay you one hundred dollars for a story or essay on baseball!"

There'd been a pause, the sound of Michael shifting his wad of gum from one side of his mouth to the other, and then the news I wanted to hear.

"Aaaah, yeah, I guess I have something." Pause. "But it's going to take me a little time to find it."

"Can you find it in a month?" I asked.

"Yeah, I think I can find it in a month. How about you send me that hundred dollars."

I did, knowing he'd have to concoct something but that he'd deliver, and it would be good. He did, and it was. But guess what he called it, this essay for a book celebrating baseball? "Why I Hate Baseball." What a punk, huh?

The essay, in fact, was something written to order not just for my *Writing Baseball* book but for this Intro to Lit class. Over the years, I'd tell Michael how students were always eager to know how much of *Season at Coole* corresponded to his real family and how his real family had turned out. Now, he took the occasion to do it, as he judged correctly that I'd be sufficiently interested in this topic to let its only partial focus on baseball get by.

The references to baseball only seem tangential: the funeral for a baseball fan, a chance meeting with Michael's brother who was the family's great baseball player, some childhood memories about playing ball, and the way, during Michael's recovery at the Smithers Institute (famous for its treatment of Mets stars Dwight Gooden and Darryl Strawberry, as well as for its help with John Cheever), he's assumed to be not a writer but a baseball star. That's why he hates baseball: because his older brother refused to coach him, selfishly keeping his talents to himself, even though Michael looks as much the player as Doc and Straw, two of our era's best.

In concluding with some news about how his real-life family turned out,

Michael would be satisfying my students' more naive curiosities. But that was not why I read it to them. Instead, like a similar essay by Alice Walker we'd be turning to week after next, it fit the pedagogy I'd learned worked so well: taking what you're not supposed to consider in literature, but which is so interesting nonetheless, and redirecting it to a proper, helpful understanding of how that literature works. *Is this story about the author? Is it really true?* In my own education, I'd been told as early as sixth grade to throw such considerations out. To raise them as an English major or graduate student would have been unthinkable. So even a first-year professor facing an intro to lit class would never have such notions on his or her mind. *But the students would.* Right there would be the initial interest. I'd only had it retaught to me by my own students at that stage, when they discovered I was working on living writers (Kurt Vonnegut, Ron Sukenick, Jerzy Kosinski), and went out and found one of their own (Jim Kunen). Why on earth sacrifice such enthusiasm? Better to use it for some momentum, showing how what was personal about literature did factor in. Having read *Season at Coole* first, my students could now feast on Michael's essay the right way, savoring not the correspondences but the differences, not the ways he'd repeated things from life but the ways he'd changed them, so they worked better for his intended effect.

Friday's class would give us another interface, our last, as we'd move from Michael Stephens (whose real-life story had sobered everyone) to Alice Walker, whose narratives deal with troubles even more devastating than alcohol and drugs. Family dysfunction is terrible, I'd warn, but national dysfunction is worse. National dysfunction? Yes, indeed. Alice Walker is an African American woman from the rural South, and most of her stories include considerations of race and gender. Black/white, male/female, rich/poor—haven't you noticed that sometimes there's a war going on out there? This was serious stuff, so even though the week was ending, I'd skip the usual joke. Actually, I'd reveal, I had run out of them. The talking dog, the platypus, the stalactite/stalagmite business, all this I'd picked up back in second grade from my brainy friend Kurt Osborn, and these three were all I could remember. How come you can only remember *bad* jokes, never good ones? Well, just as Michael Stephens had custom-written an essay for this class, so had a comedy producer out in Hollywood custom-written a joke for my students, too. But in the context of Alice Walker's first stories, it would be far from appropriate. How about we do it when we're done, which is only five class periods away? In the meantime, read the first three stories in Alice's book, *In Love and Trouble:* "Roselily," "'Really, *Doesn't*

Crime Pay?,'" and "Her Sweet Jerome." Keep this question in mind: although all three women have much in common, how are they different from each other? That's a loaded question, I admit. A majority culture tends to view minority individuals as all pretty much the same. In starting off her book, Alice wants to challenge that belief. So pay attention to how she does.

Alice Walker was the one writer on our booklist the students already knew, thanks to the popularity of *The Color Purple* as a novel and a film. But even the first time I taught her work, in the sections of Afro-American literature I did while still working with the English major curriculum of the seventies, college-age readers found her attractively accessible. "Roselily" is a good example why. It's unthreateningly short, conveniently focused, and structured by a text everyone knows by rote, the familiar words of the marriage ceremony. Its literary experiment is simple and obvious: as the minister's patented phrases hang suspended on the page, Roselily's thoughts proceed accordingly, embellishing each image with her own narrative meaning, which isn't happy. "'Really, *Doesn't* Crime Pay?'" does much same but at the other end of the social spectrum. Here a rich woman ponders the wealth her husband has provided, seeing it in a profoundly negative light because its purpose is simply to glorify her as an object. Finally, "Her Sweet Jerome" considers another kind of possession: how the woman's husband is possessed by otherwise good ideas that in his hands turn into selfishness and cruelty, mocking his wife because she is not in tune with the current Black Arts movement.

Why aren't these marriages happy? In none of them is there any great physical wrong. Indeed, all three women are pretty well off. Their husbands are, after all, doing nothing worse than being distracted. But look at the *words* Alice uses for how those distractions work on her protagonists: the joining together of Roselily's wedding seeming to be the chains of slavery, the fancy brickwork on Myrna's new home looking like cubes of raw meat, and the husband's library in Mrs. Washington's story becoming such a menace to her that she slashes and burns the books as a mortal enemy, mortal to the point of perishing with their incineration. If some of this didn't make sense in terms of simple action, it made a great impression in terms of language—something the students were by now equipped to see themselves. Even plot details had their subtleties, such as the fact that in "Her Sweet Jerome" we're never told the woman's own name—she's just called "Mrs. Jerome Washington," with only her title prefacing the husband's appellation.

Roselily submits to a marriage offering little promise of personal happiness. Mrs. Washington destroys the books (and in doing so, herself) when she finds that they're what has stolen her husband's affection. More problematic is Myrna's revenge against the husband who clothes and houses her so grandly and who wants children as a further advertisement for himself: she secretly takes birth control pills, frustrating his ambition for further trophies. Is this any less destructive than Roselily sacrificing herself into an alienating marriage (which she does for her children's sake) or Mrs. Washington burning up the books at the cost of her own life? Here is where history and a comparative sense of cultures would come in, but not as dry footnotes or the bookish analysis so common to traditional English lit courses.

To make the point, I'd remind students that the author is the great-grandchild of slaves. Hopefully, at least some in my class were lucky to have known their great-grandparents. At the age of nine months, I'd been held on my maternal great-grandfather's knee, a man born in England in 1848; plus, I have happy memories through age seven of cuddling in the lap of my paternal great-grandfather, born in Germany in 1862. Had they come from Georgia, like Alice, mine would be a different story, wouldn't it? 1848, even 1862—over in the United States at that time, slavery was being practiced, constitutional and legal. Alice Walker has to have thoughts like this, and they impact on a decision even as contemporary and as abstract as Myrna's. To thwart her oppressor, she denies a part of herself. And how much of a victory can *that* be? One thinks of slaves who'd cut off their arm to thwart their masters. It happened. In the Caribbean, in what is now the American Virgin Islands, where enslavement as a sugar cane worker was even more brutal than picking cotton or tobacco, it happened often. I've been there, seen the sites, heard the stories from great-great-grandchildren of slaves. As slave narratives became part of general American culture in the nineteenth century, such knowledge became broadly accessible. So we are fair in letting it figure in Alice's story.

At this point, we'd pause for more such considerations (you can see why we'd skip the joke this Friday). Sobered by my reminders, students would talk about their own experiences with discrimination, slavery's last remnant. Throughout, we'd emphasize how slavery itself wasn't something from the far distant past, something so far out of touch as to be an intellectualized abstraction. My mother had been born in 1911; as a little girl, when she'd see an African American as old as she was now, chances were that person had been a slave. One generation, folks—not much of a gap between me and slavery, and I'm not quite yet a fossil. Another story: I'd tell

of the little farm my wife and I were fixing up in the Shell Rock Valley, how old the limestone farmhouse was (1854, when Abolition was still an issue on which you could take sides, just like any political debate) and how one of the men hired to clean out the previous owner's junk had an interesting story of his own. His name was Willie L. Lee, a recent arrival from rural Mississippi, and as we worked together for a month, I learned lots about him. He looked to be sixty but was in fact pushing eighty (so much for my own abilities to see distinctions among minorities!). What's remarkable was that his own father had been eighty when Willie was born. That was Willie's story, and its points were family longevity and vitality, plus something else Willie obviously shared with his father: the ability of the Lee men to keep young wives, as the vibrant youth of Willie's present mate testified when she'd stop by with lunch. But as Willie L. Lee boasted of these facts, my mind was elsewhere, subtracting 160 years from today's date: I was working hand in hand, day after day in this hot Iowa summer, with the son of a slave.

Well, I was getting a great tan, too, the best I've ever had in my life. "Honey!" Mrs. Lee exclaimed to me one day toward the end, "You keep working out here, you're going to be as black as us!" I laughed back that this would be okay, but the simple fact was that it wasn't. Slavery is the one distinction in America that can never be effaced, much less erased. And here I was, sharing a last living grasp with history. I can remember not that many years ago turning on the TV news and learning that the last Civil War veteran, a drummer boy from some Confederate regiment, had just died at the age of 110 or so. A single lifetime is not much of a historical gap.

All of this is important to appreciate, I'd emphasize, but the obvious abhorrence of slavery should not lead us to regard Alice Walker as a one-dimensional writer. Just consider how she extends her sympathy—and encourages ours!—for characters not properly in synch with the new elements of black culture. It is Roselily's husband who's the culturally powerful one, yet our feelings go out to this poor, uneducated, unattractive woman who lags so pitifully behind. And just look at Jerome Washington: all the right political and cultural philosophies but applied in wrong ways. Specifically, we feel sorry for Mrs. Washington, out of style as she is, when her husband's fashionable friends make fun of her. And what does it matter that he loves black culture if that love is exercised to the exclusion of any affection for his wife, the one woman who loves him dearly, as he's the only thing she has?

We'd discuss these points not as gossip but as constructs of character.

How simple it is, we'd decide, to assume that Alice draws her protagonists in a manner reflecting her own personal affinities. Indeed, by Alice's own professional standards, it's Mr. Washington who is right and his wife who is so hopelessly behind the times that she's wrong. As a young African American writer starting out in the sixties, Alice was part of the cultural movement he espouses. All those books Mrs. Washington shreds—they're real ones, most of them good ones, and at the time, Alice Walker would have used them gratefully. In fact, it's likely that some of her own early poems, essays, stories, and novels could have been among them. This, too, will happen again and become a hallmark of Alice Walker's fiction: when it comes to being critical, she first of all criticizes herself. The Black Arts movement by itself was and is good, and Alice was and is a part of it; but it is bad when it's used to degrade and humiliate someone, as Jerome Washington III does to his wife in "Her Sweet Jerome."

This self-criticism would be an important part of our discussion Monday, when "Everyday Use" was up for consideration. There was lots to tell about Alice Walker, I'd suggest, but for now, I wanted students to read at least one more story before knowing more about her than her Georgia heritage. The piece takes place down there and concerns a mother having to decide something between her two daughters. Here's the question to keep in mind, the simplest we've had so far: Who's right, who's wrong?

Monday's class proved a good one, as the simple question provoked anything but simple answers. Of the two daughters whose rights to family heirlooms had to be decided, Dee (who'd been educated and moved up North) had her share of advocates among the students, as did Maggie, the simpler, somewhat backward sibling who'd stayed home. But for each position, there would be qualifiers, and in those qualifiers would lie the richness of the story. Butter churns, quilts—these are the objects up for debate. Dee wants them to decorate her apartment, the churn top used as an alcove table centerpiece, the quilts serving as wall hangings. True, they'll be preserved forever, whereas at home, they'd be trashed. But what else would happen with these artifacts, particularly the quilts, besides being used up? Right: they'd be used, used for what they were intended. Without the churn, how are Maggie and her mother going to make butter? And without the quilts, how will they stay warm?

True, there have been positives about Dee—it is admirable that someone could, in the old ways of saying things, pull themselves up. But didn't you find her manner pretty negative? And don't you think her desire to take these family heirlooms to the big city has something to do with show-

ing off how far she's come? She's snapping Polaroids of everything, all shots of her mother and sister including the scraggly yard, any perspectives on the simple, rude cabin framed to include the mule as well. She's taken an Islamic name, as has her accompanying boy friend; for all her efforts, the mother can't pronounce them, but she also reminds her self-taken daughter that *Dee* is not a slave name she's rejecting but the name of a beloved aunt. And there's one more thing, a subtle little touch, that shows her lack of consideration, if not downright rudeness, Yes, those monster sunglasses she keeps on all the time, indoors and out. Listen: even outdoors, if you're meeting someone face to face, having an intimate conversation, *don't* leave your sunglasses on. Slip them off, if just for introductions; and if you're a man, don't shake hands wearing gloves. This is general education; you have to learn everything here. As for Dee, it's clear she either hasn't learned or just doesn't care.

Now for Maggie: here's another of Alice Walker's patented unattractive types. The mother herself is one of these big, hefty ones, strong as an ox and able to kill and dress a hog (date material, guys?), and Maggie is the daughter taking after her. On top of it, Maggie is disfigured by burns, the ugliness of which have made her shy. The contrast with Dee, who seems to have stepped off the cover of *Vogue,* is monumental. Yet our sympathies go to Maggie, and not just because we feel sorry for her. Why so? Just because she's going to *use* these quilts? No, because on top of that, she's going to *make* them, learning from observation how bits and pieces of her family's past were not discarded but crafted back together to make something both useful and beautiful. People, you all know the quilting metaphor, have seen the AIDS quilt, have heard Jesse Jackson's quilt speech when he runs for president. This story from back in the late sixties is of quilting's rediscovery, part of its rebirth as an activity and genesis as an image for all sorts of things besides itself. Are you a poor disabled woman in the South? Don't despair: by yourself, you may be nothing, but together, you're part of the quilt! Are you an unemployed auto worker in the North with no prospects of being retrained? Don't despair: by yourself, you may be nothing, but together you're part of the quilt! It's a powerful metaphoric device, and a meaningful one. And here is one of the places it got its start.

We know by now Alice is one of these writers who uses closing emphasis, more so than Steve, whose endings have to be mechanical (as his actions would otherwise run forever), more so than Grace who wants an open-ended future for her characters. Readers inevitably perk up for endings, and as "Everyday Use" comes to a close, Alice takes advantage of this closer

attention. Has the mother done the right thing by saying no to Dee (apparently for the first time ever) and deciding Maggie will have the quilts? She loves both daughters, hates to have to choose, sincerely wants to do the right thing. Is there any evidence at the close that she has? Well, Maggie sure feels better about things, for the first time being given responsibility and, to her mother's surprised pleasure, taking responsibility from it. That's good therapy, folks. She feels good, and the mother feels good. And that's a good litmus test: if you can feel good about it afterwards, you probably did *something* right. What about us as readers, do we feel good? Probably so, as when Dee leaves, tension leaves with her. Maggie and her mother sit there in the yard for a while, the mother taking some snuff (hey guys, any of your moms use dip?) and just "enjoying" (59). Enjoying what? The sentence has no object, and for a reason: It's not so much they're enjoying Dee's absence, as they love her nonetheless, but having done the right thing, they can enjoy the fact that they're enjoying. A moment of pure bliss. Then they go inside and to bed, which is where the story ends. But as readers, we know it will be under the warm quilts.

After the sorrows and terrors of the first three stories on Friday, it would be good to spend Monday's class with a story like this, jokes about dip and all. It was fun to get the ballplayers laughing, as these guys found themselves relating to otherwise alien characters and feeling good about them. By now, everyone would be eager to learn more about Alice Walker, and there'd be plenty of time to tell she was fabulously successful now, a millionaire several times over, but ever mindful of the poverty from which she'd come. I'd tell the story of how, at age eight, she'd been wounded in the eye when her brothers were playing with BB guns, how the injury left a disfigurement that kept her shy and retiring during all those difficult years of growing up, just like Maggie. But in many respects, Alice was more like Dee, winning scholarships first to Spelman College in Atlanta (one of the traditional American Negro College Appeal universities—you know, "A Mind Is a Terrible Thing to Waste") and then to Sarah Lawrence College in suburban New York, a school at the time famous for its elite, upper-middle-class prestige. Grace Paley taught there and tried to make it funky! Its heart was in the right place, giving support to deserving students like Alice. But as any student even here at UNI knows, if you're poor, even having a full-ride scholarship doesn't mean you're home free. Think of the sacrifices Alice's family had to make just to keep her clothed and fed up there. A doctor at the college's student health service removed the cataract from her eye and ameliorated her disfigurement. She began writing po-

ems and stories, getting them published, and beginning her writer's career. But thinking back to "Everyday Use," it's important to note that for all her affinities with Maggie, Alice was still being strongly self-critical in her appraisal of Dee, for Dee's success was much more like her own. That, I'd suggest, was one of the things making her such a good writer: it's easy to criticize others, harder to criticize oneself. But Alice does it, here and in so many other stories you could read.

By now, there would be questions as to how I knew Alice Walker, especially so because she was the single writer of our four that anyone had been aware of previously. Sorry, I couldn't say she was a personal friend like Steve or Michael, not even a professional associate like Grace. But hadn't I said all the writers we were reading happened to be people I knew? Yes, to some extent I knew Alice, but not through anything I did directly. It was a student of mine who knew her, a student who brought me into the process otherwise shared with Dixon, Paley, and Stephens.

This news would be even more impressive to the average general education undergraduate than the fact that Michael Stephens had written *Season at Coole* at their age. I had to be honest: it wasn't a student in one of my Intro to Lit classes. But that didn't mean they couldn't discover someone, too. *Discover* someone like Alice Walker? *Discover* someone who a decade and a half later would have something like *The Color Purple* showing in theaters around the world, something that made Whoopi Goldberg and Oprah Winfrey famous as well? Well, my student hadn't discovered her; but he was way ahead of everyone else and did get in on the ground floor well before the author's breakthrough novel was published in 1982 and became a blockbuster film a few years after that. Consequently, I knew about Alice Walker and started teaching her way ahead of most other professors. It was a different way of getting started on her, but one more example of how working with literature works.

Who was this student? Did he or she get famous? To some extent, he did, and you've helped him amass more riches, buying the paperback edition of *Season at Coole* that his publishing house, the Dalkey Archive Press, has kept in print. He's a professor now, too, John O'Brien, but back in 1969, when I was teaching at Northern Illinois University, he was my one and only doctoral candidate. His dissertation would be a set of interviews with contemporary African American writers, and he started off seeking out the older and more famous ones (Arna Bontemps, Ann Petry, and the legendary Ralph Ellison), who in turn directed him to the less famous (Owen Dodson, John Wideman), who themselves passed along word of

the brand new, almost totally unknown figures. Among this last group was an emerging poet, novelist, and short story writer named Alice Walker, living at the time in Jackson, Mississippi, where she was supporting herself as a civil rights worker (a difficult and dangerous job, not to mention the subsistence-level pay). Jack had done a brilliant interview with her, and when he was able to publish his dissertation as *Interviews with Black Writers,* both he and Alice benefited from the exposure. Was I proud of this? You betcha! Jack dedicated the book to me. (Listen, I'd remind the class: any of you folks become famous, any of you ballplayers wind up in the World Series or Superbowl, remember where you learned it all. You want success in life? Success starts *here.*)

For Wednesday's class, we'd be considering the specific nature of Alice Walker's success. When reading "The Welcome Table," students should keep this question in mind: Is it a happy story or a sad one? That's about as easy to ask as who's right, who's wrong, and as difficult to answer. But it points up an important aspect of Alice's fame and a distinction in the ongoing history of American literature: that sentimentalism, once popular in nineteenth-century culture and looked down upon through both the modern and postmodern eras, is now once again considered okay. It's not just Alice's work, but a whole trend. You've probably heard of John Irving, whose novel *The Water Method Man* draws a large part of its setting from Iowa City, where he received his M.F.A. degree at the University of Iowa's famous Writers Workshop. You've certainly heard of UNI's Robert James Waller, well-known now for *The Bridges of Madison County* but locally prominent before that as the dean who founded our School of Business. *Bridges* has sold close to four million copies and is still going strong, not yet even in paperback. It's the most widely purchased novel of all times, passing *Gone with the Wind* some time ago. And what's its selling point? Sentimentality! Alice Walker's *Color Purple* employs sentimentality to achieve its effect; even more so, Steven Spielberg's movie, which had me crying my eyes out. That kind of response used to be abominated, but now it's very much in vogue, because literary culture has evolved with popular tastes. And some of the first evidence of it, before John Irving and well before Bob Waller, can be found in stories Alice wrote as a very young woman back in the late sixties and early seventies. So, there's your assignment: read "The Welcome Table" and give some thought to whether it's happy or sad.

Come Wednesday, reactions would be spirited, some readers thinking it sad (because the old black woman is given a gentle version of the bum's

rush out of the white church she wishes to attend), while others insisting that it's a happy ending, given how she dies with a vision of the person she's been seeking, Jesus. Well, is this what really happens at the end? Is Alice insisting on a religious interpretation? Not at all. Look at all the disclaimers in that last paragraph, how the perspective draws back to consider what some people *thought* they saw, what the woman *seemed to be doing*— "Silly as it seemed," we're told, given every chance to opt out of believing. Yet with all those hedgings, we're left with the implication that whether real or not, the old woman felt her vision was genuine—and consequently, she dies happily. So you don't have to be a Christian to accept the ending. Alice makes that allowance. But she also hints that the old black woman has been seeking Jesus in the wrong place. If you are a Christian, and a sincere one, do you think Jesus was present in that hypocritical white church? Or is he out there on the road with the old, dying lady?

With Friday's class free for groups to work on their papers, I'd look ahead to Monday's class with the same question for "Strong Horse Tea": Is it a happy story or a sad one? Then, to finish up our discussions on Wednesday, read "To Hell with Dying" and see if Alice was holding out any hope, any possibilities that somewhere in life were situations beyond the unhappiness seen in so much of her work.

With papers in mind, I'd take some time to repeat what I was seeking— not summaries but analysis, not just Harry Caray or Pat Summerall's play-by-play but Steve Stone or John Madden's explanation of *why* the play happened that way, *how* it was designed, *what* went right or wrong, *where* specific things were beginning, developing, and finding their resolutions. The approach shouldn't be overly formal, nor should you have to reinvent the wheel at each turn—you can assume we all know the stories, so get right to the point. With that understood, you could get a lot of interesting work done in a five-page paper. But do remember that even at this late date, the vast majority of your time should be spent thinking about the issues of comparison and contrast, talking about them if you're doing the paper as a group. You're not just reciting facts, like running through the rules of tennis, but rather working with literature, analogous to playing a set out there on the clay court. You've been reactive in your first exposure to these stories; now be proactive, as has happened when we've gone into deeper discussions.

Monday's class would begin the home stretch of Introduction to Literature. "Strong Horse Tea" poses a greater challenge to discover something

happy, as its central event is the death of a little baby. In struggling to find some positives, students would offer that perhaps the kid was better off out of its suffering, better off out of a life of abysmal, even dire poverty and deprivation. But at the same time, we had to admit that these were pretty lame excuses; overwhelming all else was the sense that of all possible deaths, the death of a baby is the cruelest, saddest, and most unforgivable of mortalities, especially since this particular death is unnecessary. Double pneumonia and whooping cough can kill you, particularly if you're very young or very old, but they don't have to. Each is treatable. Isn't that one of the saddest aspects of this story, that the mother has all the best intentions, is being a responsibly good mother by insisting a doctor see the child, but that her plea for help is never even conveyed? Yes, it's happening in a context of prejudice, discrimination, isolation, primitive conditions, and rock-bottom poverty. But even here, we'd like to think no physician would deny care to a dying baby. The problem is that the message never gets through.

As Monday's class proceeded, we would discuss the dynamics of the story's first incident, where Rannie Toomer, anxious for her baby's health, flags down the mailman and asks him to send word. We know what Rannie's saying, because Alice tells us. But what is the letter carrier hearing? Not a word. All he can think of is how dirty, ignorant, and incoherent the woman is, and probably ugly as well. Just stop leaning into my car, lady, he seems to be thinking, you're going to mess it up. Here is one more of Alice Walker's women, awkward and unattractive, getting the cold shoulder from an indifferent world. Consider how different the scene would be were she blessed with the looks and personality of, say, Janet Jackson or Whitney Houston or any such star. Why, that mailman would order up a limo! "Miss *Jackson,* what can I *do* to *help* you?" Think, too, how easy it would be for us to sympathize. That we do feel sorry for her, ugly and all, is to our credit. It certainly helps us understand why her baby is the world to her, for the child is the only thing in this life she has.

What about the old root-worker's advice, that Rannie treat the sick child with "strong horse tea"? Here, I'd step back from the story's misery to tease a bit, saying that inevitably there'd be someone in class who didn't know what the substance was. Was it the sweat from a horse? When that was once suggested, I said, I felt sorry for the student's embarrassment. So to save any such confusion now, would someone say what strong horse tea really was? "Horse piss!" the ballplayers would chorus, and amidst the laughs,

I'd reason that urine is always good for a few jokes—such as when the lab test run on the brew from a college-days kegger I attended came back saying, "We're sorry to report that your horse has diabetes."

Is it possible the horse urine will help the child? Such ammoniac properties can clear sinuses, but that doesn't seem to be what Alice is getting at. What is her purpose? Well, how does she describe Rannie's quest for the substance? Look: it's monumental, chasing the untethered horse across a plowed field, all muddy, with rain and sleet and lightning and thunder crashing down. When she finally gets the urine, she has nothing to put it in but her cracked plastic shoe, which she must hold to her mouth so the liquid doesn't leak out, Why does Alice do this to her character? Hasn't the poor young mother suffered enough? Can doing this possibly help the baby?

Probably not. Right at the start, the infant has been described as lying as still as in a grave, so the odds aren't good. Yet perhaps the task is not for the baby's benefit, but for the mother's. At her wits' end, it gives her something to do. And given that the baby is almost surely lost, at least the mother can never blame herself that she didn't try everything, didn't go to the full extent of her strength. And, most important for us, it allows readers to sympathize with an otherwise unattractive character. Yes, the world is filled with misery. But there's a chance for improvement when people like us can feel our hearts going out to a character we might otherwise prefer not to think about.

As we'd get ready to conclude our work on Alice Walker and wind up the course, I'd ask students to consider if the stories of *In Love and Trouble* were taking a direction toward hopefulness. One thing you can do, I counseled, is check to see if the author has arranged them in some other order than in which they were written—consult the library's periodical indices, for example, for each piece's date of publication. See if the author has written essays and given interviews. Or drop the person a note yourself. You'd be surprised how often he or she will answer.

As for an emerging sense of hope, that's what I'd ask students to look for in "To Hell with Dying." As the last day's discussion began, we'd mention the obvious facts of the story: an old man dies, but happily, surrounded by those who have loved him. Is there any special way we get there? By looking at the language, and specifically at the initial grammar of the narrative, we'd see the writing style itself grows up along with the storyteller, from a sing-song, run-on, uncritical recitation of the old man's qualities and faults to the way he helps this once-little girl develop a sense of es-

teem about herself. Summoned from graduate school to his deathbed, she's enveloped in a joy of happy senses: the smell of roses outside the window, the feel of the muslin sheets on his bed, the sound of his guitar, on which he'd played that most unthreatening of songs from African American culture, the Harlem Globetrotter's theme, "Sweet Georgia Brown." And what does she learn from this? That this old gentleman had been her first love.

"Love," I'd mention—is this the first time in the entire book that the word's been used in all its positive connotations? Think about it: isn't this the first example, right at the book's very end, of untroubled love between a man and a woman? True, he's ancient and infirm, no threat at all to a woman. It's not much. But, as *In Love and Trouble* closes, it's at least a start. And Alice only allows that start after having us realize all the troubles in the stories that went before. If we as readers want some sentimental love, we have to earn the right to it. By the end of her book, we have. That's why if you feel a few tears coming, it's okay.

Now, what about this essay I am going to use to make everyone cry? This would be appropriate for the last class, as it was something Alice Walker wrote about the real-life background for "To Hell with Dying."

In teaching literature, the most frequent question I'd get, more frequently in introductory classes, was to what extent the narrative was real. Did this really happen to the author? Or, to put it with a bit more sophistication (while still asking essentially the same thing), what were the author's influences for writing this way about this material? John Irving, one of the writers I'd identified as marking the return to honest sentimentalism in fiction, has two of his characters in *The World According to Garp* consider the issue. Garp, a novelist himself, tells his kids a story, then concludes it— with striking modifications—for his wife. The kids assume it is autobiographical, but Helen Garp, who's an English professor, knows that it is mostly made up. Yet even she demands a coherent model, insisting that in her husband's imaginative creation of a tale there be a standard of internal truth. Seeing so many parts change confuses her. "Which of it is true," she asks, "and which of it is made up?" Garp plays it as a game with her, always giving the same answer: "Every part she believed was true; every part she didn't believe needed work" (193).

There's much of the "Garp" method to Alice Walker's work, I'd now show, pulling out an essay called "Remembering Mr. Sweet" she'd published in *The New York Times Book Review* and collected in her volume called *Living by the Word,* where it appears as "The Old Artist: Notes on Mr. Sweet."

Short enough to read aloud in four or five minutes, it's an engaging and soon powerful piece, telling readers (even in their total lack of sophistication) exactly what they want to know: what happened in real life, and which parts of it needed more work to become a successful piece of fiction.

There *was* an old man back home whom everyone called "Mr. Sweet." His real name was Mr. Little, but the nickname fit him better, so even among Alice's friends and family, the fictive process had begun. In terms of his failures, he was actually a bit worse than the story's creation; on top of the drinking, my students could now marvel that he was a gambler and a reckless handler of firearms as well. But the little kids loved him as in the story, expressed in the essay by Alice's one clear memory of him, sitting in her grandmother's kitchen while biscuits and gravy-smothered chicken were being prepared, playing guitar and singing. That he's tipsy at the time doesn't matter, because he is such a beneficially soulful artist. Alice's elders teach her to respect him and his words and his music.

That's the first page. Then he dies. As was her protagonist in the story, Alice is up North when it happens—not doing a doctorate but simply finishing her B.A. degree at Sarah Lawrence College in Westchester, New York. But there's a departure from details even larger than this, because in the essay, it turns out that Alice has been feeling alienated and depressed in this rich, white environment. Moreover, she doesn't have the money to go home, even though it's the Christmas holidays. Instead, she spends the break with a friend, and on the day of Mr. Sweet's funeral writes the story we've just read, with tears streaming down her face, with the razorblade she'd been ready to use on her wrists set aside.

Every time I'd come to this part, I couldn't help feeling stunned, and the class would be stunned with me. It would be hard to continue, but I'd read on through Alice's explanation of why *she* was continuing, finding the strength to be an artist in Mr. Sweet's example, the example of having taken the trials and even terrors of his life and transformed them into art, art that could be shared with others. Through it all, *he continued to sing.* Now Alice would, too, even as she fought for her life.

On just the third page, this essay came to an end, where the author recalls how her memory of Mr. Sweet saving her was the first story she ever published. But it wasn't the first one she'd ever written. The title of that first one, never to my knowledge published (because it didn't need to be published), was "The Suicide of an American Girl."

General education classes aren't supposed to have moments like these. But the students had been warned, and seven weeks of ups and downs with

the other writers had them ready. We'd discuss the implications of Alice's essay, building from the good her story did for her to the good it does for readers, even readers who don't know the background. We'd think back to some of the more serious things Dixon, Paley, and Stephens had done with their literary art and consider how we might answer that most naive of questions. Is this true? Is that true? Yes, if it works on you. Happily, most of the literature we'd read did.

But one couldn't end a semester like this, nor should students be sent off to write their papers in such an emotionally traumatized mood. That's why I'd promised a joke, a joke that would elevate feelings. I mean really elevate them, making the day's experience a roller-coaster ride of emotions. There was a pedagogical reason for this: all through the course, I'd told these intentionally bad jokes but would now "revise" one to flatter their discrimination as critics. Working with literature drew on the same techniques as doctoring jokes, and I could present a valid experience of having been involved with just that. I could tell a story about it, and everyone loves hearing a story, particularly after a shock like they'd just had.

There was this guy I know, I'd explain, named Bob Weide, who's a producer out in Los Angeles, a comedy producer, doing HBO specials for Billy Crystal and creating documentaries for public TV. His Marx Brothers program won a public broadcasting award, and his show on W. C. Fields won an Emmy, all before he was thirty. Recently, he'd begun work on novelist Kurt Vonnegut's humor. As Vonnegut was one of my special interests, Bob had sought me out and hired me as a consultant. So I'd be in touch with him every few weeks for something about the project.

One Friday, he'd phoned me right after class and found me in a down mood. What was wrong? Well, I'd told this joke that hadn't gone over very well. What was the joke? I told him the Famous Talking Dog Joke, which he received in silence, taking some time before he said, "I see your problem." But he claimed he could solve it. After all, comedy was his business, fixing jokes something he did as a profession. He'd even been on "Letterman" with his own material. Redoing the Famous Talking Dog Joke into something that would work was easy. Just give him a few minutes, let him toss it around in the back of his mind while we discussed some things about Kurt Vonnegut. We did this, and as promised, he wound up our phone call with a makeover of my lame piece of humor. Now it was the Revised Talking Dog Joke, and it went like this.

Guy walks into a bar, sits down. Dog runs in after him, sits down on the next bar stool. You can tell they're together because the guy's wearing

a blue stocking cap, the dog's wearing a blue stocking cap. The bartender sees this, comes over, and tells the guy to get this mutt outta here, this is a bar, not a menagerie.

"But bartender," the guy says, "this is no mutt! This is the Famous Talking Dog!"

"I don't care no Famous Talking Dog," the bartender replies. "Get him *out* or you're both going to go flying through the door!"

"Please," the guy begs, "let me prove it to you. In fact, I'll bet you ten dollars my dog can talk!"

"Okay," the bartender says, "I'll take your ten dollars before I toss you out of here. Put your money there, and you're on."

The guy does, turns to his dog, and says, "Spot"—that's the dog's name, Spot—"what's on top of a house?" (Knowing looks would have begun spreading across faces from the moment I said the first line, and the familiarity of the joke's rhythms took us back to that first Friday class seven weeks ago. So far, not one part of the joke had changed. But the students and I had changed, they knowing a lot more about how literature worked, me knowing at least a few things about them, and all of us veterans of some pretty pathetic attempts at humor. But with the promise of something different, an improvement, they were eager to see how, when, why, and where it would happen. This is what the last seven weeks had been about; this is what they were now trained to do.)

The dog pulls himself up a bit, clears his throat, and says, "Ah, *architecture,* a complex and demanding topic. What's on top of a house? Why, there could be many things, from a cantilevered structure to a system of arch supports to an air-supported inflatable ceiling such as we have on our own university sports arena here in Cedar Falls. But to make it simple and at the same time universal, let me say that what's on top of a house is a *roof!*"

(Class reaction would be wonderful; the joke was half-way redeemed already, thanks not to anything in it itself but because we were having fun contrasting it to what they'd heard so many weeks before, what they'd not really understood at the time. Now they did, and that made for pleasure, if not outright humor. But they hoped, with reason, that something genuinely funny was coming. It's just that they had no idea *what.* Just wait, my manner implied.)

"Holy cow," the bartender exclaims, "this dog is great. Buddy, you've won your ten dollars. Plus have a beer on me!"

"Hey," the guy says, "we'll do another one for free. This is a sports bar, right? Let me ask Spot here a question about sports."

He turns to the dog and says "Spot, who was the most famous New York Yankee of all times?"

The dog sits up like he's thinking, clears his throat, and says "Ah, the New York Yankees, baseball's most fabled franchise, the dynasty of dynasties. Even down to the present moment, we can name great Gotham heroes, but for the grandest, we have to go back. To Mickey Mantle? Farther than that, to Joe Dimaggio? Well, if you ask me, I'd have to return to that fantastic team of 1927 and work my way down Murderers' Row until I got to the great Bambino, the Sultan of Swat, the one and only Babe *Ruth!*"

(Into it now, students would be applauding but also eager for the punch line, as they knew from the original that there was a major part yet to cover. After all, they were now well-trained literary critics.)

Now the bartender's even more impressed, gives the guy another beer on the house, and invites him to get comfortable and enjoy the fruits of his labors. A talking dog! What a great example of what you can teach man's best friend to do! So the guy finishes his second beer, has a third, and pretty soon has to answer nature's call. He's only in the men's room a few minutes, but when he comes back, Spot's gone, and their places have been cleared.

"Hey, bartender!" he calls in a panic. "Where's Spot, where's my Famous Talking Dog?"

"The dog?" he's told. "Oh, when you were in the john, a French poodle came in, sat down next to your friend, and started talking, and a few minutes later they left together."

Even more panicked now, the guy dashes out the door and looks up and down the street. What he sees, though, is right at his feet. There, out on the sidewalk, Spot and the French poodle are doing what only dogs would do in public, you know. (You bet the class knew but were nevertheless stunned that an off-color joke was going to be told in class. Talk about an emotional roller coaster—there were still damp eyes from Alice Walker's essay, and now *this*. I could keep it clean, keep a distance from any vulgarity but still get the effect—and these sharply proficient critics could tell that.)

"Spot!" the guy exclaims. "This is disgusting, this is revolting! I've never seen you do anything so terrible before!"

Spot looks back over his shoulder, considers his master's complaint, and says, "Well, I've never had ten dollars before!"

So much of the joke and its particular telling depend upon context: that it's done in class, that it's done in contrast to the original telling, that it takes its place in a series of other jokes that in innocence and purity seem

quaint. As jokes I'd heard in second grade, they *were* quaint. This new one was anything but, and what it was happened to be very adult. Told as it was at the end of our class, after Alice Walker's essay but also after all her stories and the narratives by our other writers, it marked a passage for the students, a passage into the collegiality of working critics.

Now, the class would be sent off to finish writing papers. They'd had sample questions to consider since the start, had been dealing with them at least casually for the past several weeks, and now had the equivalent of two full meetings to write them. As so many were group projects, common time was a necessity; but even for the solitary writers, I wanted plenty of room available. Each student had at least five other courses to contend with, I'd have to remember, just as in my own life there were always half a dozen various things going on, from mowing the lawn or shoveling snow to various professional and social life duties and just plain enjoyment. When I had to write something important, I did not try to do a seventh or eighth thing on top of it but rather pulled back from as much as I could. And as a new-generation graduate director would say almost two decades later, I did not go and lock myself into a room for two hours with nothing but pencils and a bluebook to write it. Therefore, Friday and Monday's class times would be free for doing the paper's final draft. I'd be available in my office those hours if anyone wanted help. Folks would come—almost always those who didn't need it. Isn't it true that the only students who worry about their final grades are the ones who don't have to worry? But the truth was that students, as many as half the class, just wanted to come by and visit. We'd talk about their papers for a while and then chat about anything from baseball to their backgrounds and their hopes for the future until someone else showed up outside the door. All in all, it was a very pleasant way to wind up our otherwise intensive half-semester.

With just a few exceptions, the papers that came in were good. The sample questions I'd proposed and the self-generated ones I'd approved were promptings toward simple comparison-and-contrast essays. Initial references were grounded in content but answerable only by moving into matters of technique, so the results were virtually guaranteed to be analytical. Except for Michael Stephens, we'd read a variety of material by each author, and with Michael, it had been a full novel, complemented by my summary of his baseball essay and a description of his play, "Our Father," in which seven brothers leave their dad's funeral with the old man's corpse and coffin, take it to the corner tavern, and spend the evening drinking

and telling stories (the father sits up for some beers and storytelling, too). It's important, I think, that if someone is going to write on a couple authors, they have a comfortable familiarity with their work; how anyone can write coherently with just anthologized snippets (from several score authors!) escapes me. Happily, we were all sufficiently comfortable with Dixon, Paley, Stephens, and Walker that choosing two to write on made for an intelligent pick, and comparing and contrasting the pair on a specific point seemed a natural project to undertake.

How do two of the writers handle women characters? To what extent are determinants of region, economics, social setting, and so forth significant in their fiction? A dozen such topics would easily come to hand, and after discussing these writers in such detail, there would be an eagerness to put two of them together and see what might happen. The method was still inductive. I was not asking my students to look over sixty Petrarchan sonnets by twenty-some authors and another sixty or seventy Elizabethan sonnets by a score or so more authors and tell me what was the reductive difference. For the Intro to Lit papers, there were no correct answers to deduce; if there had been, I simply would have presented them on day one and saved us all seven and a half weeks' work. The work they'd do in these papers was more properly a hands-on affair, working *with* the literature itself rather than manipulating ideas about it.

Now it was Wednesday, the course's last meeting (we could have done this on the subsequent Friday, but with other classes ending and a weekend looming, such would be counterproductive for the results I wanted). I would not be there for the first ten minutes, for this was the time for the class evaluation, administered by one of the department secretaries. My evaluations have always been high. A few of the closing questions solicited discursive answers. In these personal comments were the best rewards. I won't summarize all of them or even gloat about a few. Let it suffice to quote just one, a very representative one: "I learned more in this one class," a graduating senior confided, "than I have in all of my other college classes put together."

With the secretary's departure, I'd come in, thank the students for their trouble with the evaluation, and ask about their papers. Before collecting them and heading home for a couple days' reading, I wanted to know how they'd handled the task. What was easy about it? What was hard? What should I take into account when reading the papers? What were some of their approaches? It was better for me to have a general sense of this now;

otherwise, the first paper would be read in such a different context from the last one. I'd hear confirmation that it was indeed harder to write a group paper than an individual one—but less lonely and more stimulating, so the trade-off was fair. I'd hear how the hardest task wasn't finding information but knowing what of the obvious surplus to discard. I'd hear all the things a veteran instructor tells his or her composition classes; the pleasant difference was that in this case, the students had learned it all themselves in the process of doing the assignment. Self-instructed, the lessons would last. All that extra time for the papers had been worth it.

Then, before collecting the work, I'd make a few closing announcements. One was that this course was like a Midas muffler: it had a lifetime warranty. In coming semesters, if anyone needed some advice or inside knowledge about other courses and teachers at the university, feel free to ask. You know me now—I'll be candid. Further on, say five or ten years from now, you might be wondering if Steve Dixon ever got famous or his wife's health improved, if Michael Stephens was still a punk, and so forth. By the late eighties, I could begin telling about one of Intro to Lit's more interesting warranty calls—from Marcus Weems, who as a student in the first time 'round with *In Love and Trouble* had read Alice Walker well ahead of *The Color Purple*'s movie craze and wanted me to affirm that fact to his mother. That Marcus was now aged thirty and director of a major social service agency apparently wasn't credibility enough for Mom. "See," I'd advise, "a teacher can still help you years on." Then, there was a call I got from a student nearly twenty years past, wondering if I'd be in Chicago the coming summer. No, the drive and the traffic were putting me off these days. Well, he was vice-president of an ad agency on Wacker Drive, one of the city's biggest and best firms, and they had a season-ticket field box at Wrigley Field . . ."In circumstances like this," I'd advise, "help becomes a two-way street, so don't forget me when you've made it big."

I'd promised no more than a half-hour class, and as the time came, I could tell students were thinking of their other obligations; I'd told them they'd have the rest of this semester-ending hell to concentrate on other classes, and they were ready to take me up on it. But I couldn't let them leave without a couple more jokes. My excuse would be that in reviewing the semester, I'd realized there were two things I'd forgotten to teach them, important things in general education's preparation for life. One involved knowing how to sleep through classes and still get passing grades. Obviously, this wasn't a talent I would have shared with them on day one, but

now that they'd acquired nearly everything else and the class was ending, why not learn the trick? It was a device perfected by F. Scott Fitzgerald when he was a student at Princeton, who for three years burned both ends of the candle at drama club and parties yet stayed alive by getting his sleep during classes and kept from flunking out by virtue of something very clever indeed.

"Here's what you do," I'd instruct. "Get your sleep in big classes where you can be somewhat unobtrusive in the last row." But even in big classes, profs catch on to this, students would object, and spot you out with questions. Then you *are* in trouble, because on top of being caught sleeping, you're exposed as not knowing the material.

"Fitzgerald had that part of it solved," I'd confide. "When the prof would waken him with a question, he'd say, 'Sir, do you mean that objectively or subjectively?' Nine times out of ten, the professor would not only repeat the question but become intrigued by the distinction and answer it himself, crediting the intelligence to Fitzgerald."

Didn't I realize some of the ballplayers had been pulling that on me the last seven weeks?

"Okay," I'd scoff, "go take your passing grade and write *The Great Gatsby*. At the very least, read *The Great Gatsby*, which has lots of lessons about all sorts of things."

The other lesson for life involved how to handle a potentially large check when you had to take someone out to dinner. The answer? Show up at the door with a candy bar. Chances are the person is going to be pretty hungry, and that snack will look good. If your date or your boss or whomever you're treating objects, especially if you've laid on a three-pound Hershey's Symphony Bar or something like that, just say, "But you're the *greatest!*" Then, if that doesn't do it, swing past Baskin-Robbins on the way and get a triple-scoop cone. Rocky Road is especially filling. Then go to dinner, where your date or your boss will probably just order a salad, and you're out of there for six bucks.

Amid the chuckles and groans, I'd call for the papers, thank the students for their work, and excuse myself to go off and start reading. Some of the folksier in the class would stick around to chat. Every few semesters, there would be a student who asked about becoming an English major, confessing that Intro to Lit had made a whole lot more sense than accounting or computer studies. I'd warn them away, saying that there was precious little in the English major like Intro to Lit and absolutely nothing in the man-

ner with which this class had been taught. Why weren't all English courses like this? I could not break an eager heart by telling why. What I'd do in these circumstances is just say it was such a great job, such a great privilege, to teach a course like Intro to Lit that there were all sorts of hoops you had to jump through first. "Like becoming the captain of United Airlines' flight to Hawaii?" a student might ask, and I'd have to say, "Yes."

Afterword

This book was begun on a spring semester sabbatical set aside for writing a narratological study of World War II air combat memoirs, which itself justified professional travel to Pearl Harbor and the rest of Hawaii. By March, however, the book was already done, so I used the rest of my time (and the amenities of a little rented house on the grounds of a former guava plantation on Kauai) to write my first chapter about being so incorrectly educated in literature. Over the summer and fall, I took time away from fixing up our little quasi farm in the country to write an account of my "home schooling." When my customary second half-semester pair of sections in Intro to Lit started October 21, I began setting aside each Monday-Wednesday-Friday morning to write about the class as it transpired. After a month, I couldn't keep up the pace; even with six or seven pages on each meeting, there was no way I could but scratch the surface of what was happening in the classroom. So over Christmas break, I caught up with the teaching of Michael Stephens and Alice Walker, finishing the Sunday morning before Monday's first half of spring semester begins, as always, with my two sections of Intro to Lit running through the end of February. On March 1, I go back to full-time research, doing a study of American culture surrounding World War II that I trust will be winding up when I visit some old air bases in England before starting up class again the third week of October. It's a tough job, but somebody has to do it, right?

The important question, however, is the one so many students have asked me—business students, industrial technology students, students who are more passionate about getting an answer the farther away from the humanities they happen to be: Why aren't all English classes like this? The cruel answer is that they aren't because an entire industry has been built up whose vastness depends upon teaching literature the wrong way. That the major and the profession continue to crumble seems not to dissuade its practitioners. Every year, there are more and more required courses.

From an English major that was once thirty hours, new requirements have bumped it up to nearly seventy full credits. To the dead weight of history have been added the cement overshoes of theory; and if, as with so many majors at a school like the University of Northern Iowa, teaching certification is to be attached, you can expect state legislature-mandated courses in everything from soil conservation to the benefits of eating vast quantities of pork and beef. Every year, there are fewer English majors, and those there are seem duller and dumber. Meanwhile, the brightest minds seem to be in business and industrial tech, where literature—when properly taught—is feasted upon. Many of my colleagues, repulsed by the fact that these accounting and computer engineering grads will be earning at age twenty-two more than they themselves make at fifty, consider such a general ed lit course a waste of time. I ask them if they so despise rich folks (and the future rich) that they'd deny them an education in anything other than technologies. But deeper than economic jealousies run the prejudices against a happy (rather than grim) work ethic: if the teacher and the students are getting so much enjoyment out of this course, it obviously shouldn't exist. Literature involves pleasure? To the drudges caught in their downward spirals of a dying profession, the notion is inconceivable.

I hope this book will demonstrate how my profession's negativity has sentenced it to preordained failure. My own solution has been eminently personal. Thanks to my salary, rank, and publication record, I was able to write my own ticket for classes and schedules. That alone is not exceptional; indeed, having the chance to do so provides the standard incentive among university professors in all fields. But where so many profs, when given the chance, disappear into an esoteric doctoral seminar focused on the minutiae of their research, I've been close to unique in devoting 100 percent of my teaching to the entry-level (some would say "bonehead") lit class for everyone but English majors. Some would object that doing this might cripple my own research efforts. Again, on a personal level, the result has been anything but. Teaching one basic course but with an infinitely varied curriculum lets me, under the general umbrella of "literature" (which is what the course is all about!), quite literally do whatever I want. New books and new writers fit in naturally, as do new ideas. During the twenty years I've taught Intro to Lit almost exclusively, I've published books on Peter Handke's postmodernism, Roland Barthes's poststructuralism, jazz musician Gerry Mulligan's aural sensibilities, several volumes of my own fiction, and any number of litcrit topics, plus narratological volumes on how flyers in the various theaters of World War II told their stories. All

this work finds its genesis in my teaching and returns there for its application. Of course, in the Intro to Lit classroom, it has to at least start out with common intelligibility. Rather than come in loaded for bear with theories about semiotics, I'd point to the magnetic lettering displayed out there in front of the Dairy Queen, where last week, instead of advertising a special on Dilly Bars, the message read, "Dana said to change the sign, so I did." There's self-referentiality for you. Deconstruction? How about the greeting card I'd bought my wife for her thirtieth: "Happy birthday," it read; "today is the first day of what's left of your life." See? Change two little words, and the sentiment comes completely apart. Meanwhile, as my books on Handke and Barthes and others appeared, they'd get good reviews or bad, but even the bad ones would admit my clarity. When you're talking with business and industrial tech majors every other day, you damned well better be clear.

Do I have a plan for the literature curriculum beyond the personal? Yes, I do, and from time to time I urge it among friends—and as the bitter old failures have retired and been replaced with bright and eager (and competent!) young assistant professors, there's been a lot more friendship in my department. It involves dismantling the rusting curricular industry, but few of them have a vested interest in it, educated as they've been in methods beyond priestly New Criticism and pontifical literary history.

How we'd all do it could be simple and would get the lit major back down to a proper thirty hours. Yes, a literature major—departments should stop saying they're willing to do the job high schools neglected in teaching basic composition and admit that such skills should have already been perfected by sixth grade. No wonder secondary education can't do it and doesn't want to. Besides, my own class showed me with good fiction as a model, students could pick up ideas about how to write decently, particularly when they had to thrash it out among themselves. Maybe the technique is a bit off-the-deep-end-of-the-swimming-pool, but total immersion in narrative never asphyxiated anyone. Let comp happen naturally, with more models and affinitive exercises as in Intro to Lit, rather than have students argue over issues like abortion and capital punishment, then write contrived essays. Let them analyze how actual writers like Michael Stephens and Alice Walker handle situations that beg to be told about. Understanding how literature works is not a specialty, much less the doings of a secret society. It is a basic human activity, and English majors (despite so many efforts spent to the contrary) are human.

With Intro to Lit and a comp-intensive class, the English department

would offer eight other courses, some of which could be elective: a two-semester survey of American literature, a complementary pair of courses on English and British writing, at least two courses on literature written in English but outside the culturally and historically dominant main-streams, and introductory and advanced creative writing classes. The major would also draw on electives from other departments, including the Department of Languages (in translation) and the Department of History (for larger grounding). Missing would be the specifically historical special-izations (Early Milton, Early Middle Milton, Middle Milton, Late Middle Milton, Little Milton, and so on) and even period concentrations (the Vic-torian Novel, American Romanticism, and others).

Well, the traditionalists say, there goes the English major. But it goes somewhere other than out the window. It goes into the M.A. and Ph.D. degrees, where specialization has its place. The idea of first-semester sopho-mores testing out of prerequisites so they can, at age nineteen, dive into Cavalier Poetry or Restoration Drama (or Middle Late Milton) is prepos-terous, unless you've got such a protopedant on your hands that he or she has left life in the practical world almost totally behind—in which case you're looking at a terrible prospect for appreciating a Grace Paley story, much less the Revised Famous Talking Dog Joke. Until recently, there have been enough of them to fill the standard curriculum's classrooms and keep those classes staffed. But with the millennium's end, their numbers are shrinking, even as the literature they deal with fails to survive. At Marquette University in the early sixties, I saw the last gasp of Latin as a dead lan-guage yet still living pedagogy, a pedagogy on the last cycle of support kept going simply because 1 or 2 percent of its students would join the Jesuit order (and need it there). The traditional English major seems in similar shape now. Anything other than composition and introductory genre sur-veys are offered interchangeably with graduate-level courses, analogical not just to the single future priest learning Latin but to the very old days of professional baseball, where a dozen ascending classes of minor leagues would have twenty-four nonprospects playing catch with the single ath-lete likely to progress. Surely, there must be some purpose for offering an undergraduate English major beyond letting future doctoral candidates get a portion of their required course work completed. And just look at the style of academic politics such a curriculum breeds, where souls that should be lofty and pure for dealing with special achievement become poisoned by the noxious business of turf wars.

Much in the standard curriculum fails the purpose of literature, which is to provide artistically written expression, in a culture's common language, of its most imaginative thoughts. Too many existing courses, sectioned off historically as they are, have to spend too much time scaling barriers of diction and usage; worst of all, the barriers sometimes become a subject of their own, an end in itself, a self-contained Egyptology of interest only to its narrow masters. It's no accident that such literature lived on in late-twentieth-century college classrooms largely as examples for deconstruction, a method that has grown into its own Egyptology of sorts. What's lost is the sense of people reading literature for the reasons literature was invented.

My examples have been directly personal, because that's how I retaught myself how to handle lit classes in an effective way. To those who might say I've really benefited from an old-fashioned education, let me remind them that what was in fact my miseducation—as an English major fine tuned in graduate school to study nineteenth-century American writing—was from the second semester of my first appointment left behind. If someone tries calling me a specialist in modern and contemporary fiction, I cite the facts that I had just one undergraduate class and a single grad course on the subject, failed the area on my doctoral comprehensives, and only got into it when my students showed me how fascinating it was to work with living authors. It's no accident that my work in the field is so noticeably different from that of other scholars, not in the least because it is readable by nonspecialists and of interest to those who simply love literature and everything about it.

What I do know for certain is that literature itself hasn't died. It is just being taught the wrong way in the wrong place. In my Intro to Lit sections, I've handled it not as a product but as a process, to the delight of the university's brightest and most responsible students. There's no way English majors can't have it this way, too.

Bibliography

Barthelme, Donald. "Porcupines at the University." *New Yorker* 46 (April 25, 1970): 32–33. Collected with changes in *Amateurs*. New York: Farrar, Straus & Giroux, 1976, 113–21.

———. "Snap Snap." *New Yorker* 41 (August 28, 1965): 108, 110–11. Collected in *Guilty Pleasures*. New York: Farrar, Straus & Giroux, 1974, 31–37.

———. *Snow White*. New York: Atheneum, 1967.

Coover, Robert. "The Babysitter." In *Pricksongs & Descants*. New York: Dutton, 1969, 206–39.

Dixon, Stephen. *14 Stories*. Baltimore: Johns Hopkins University Press, 1980.

———. *Interstate*. New York: Henry Holt, 1995.

———. *Quite Contrary: The Mary and Newt Story*. New York: Harper & Row, 1979.

———. *Time to Go*. Baltimore: Johns Hopkins University Press, 1985.

Faulkner, William. *Knight's Gambit*. New York: Random House, 1949.

———. *The Reivers*. New York: Random House, 1962.

Fitzgerald, F. Scott. *The Vegetable*. New York: Scribner's, 1923.

Irving, John. *The World According to Garp*. New York: Dutton, 1978.

Jones, LeRoi [Amiri Baraka]. *Blues People*. New York: Morrow, 1963.

Klinkowitz, Jerome. *The American 1960s: Imaginative Acts in a Decade of Change*. Ames: Iowa State University Press, 1980.

———. *Basepaths*. Baltimore: Johns Hopkins University Press, 1995.

———. *The Life of Fiction*. Urbana: University of Illinois Press, 1977.

———. *Literary Disruptions: The Making of a Post-Contemporary American Fiction*. Urbana: University of Illinois Press, 1975.

———. *Owning a Piece of the Minors*. Carbondale: Southern Illinois University Press, 1999.

———. "Pieces of Peace: A Letter to Local Board 18, Selective Service System, Framingham, Massachusetts, on Behalf of James Simon Kunen." *North American Review* 258 (Spring 1973): 67–70.

———, ed. *Writing Baseball*. Urbana: University of Illinois Press, 1991.

Klinkowitz, Jerome, and John Somer, eds. *Innovative Fiction*. New York: Dell, 1972.

————. *The Vonnegut Statement.* New York: Delacorte Press/Seymour Lawrence, 1973.

Kunen, James Simon. *The Strawberry Statement: Notes of a Student Revolutionary.* New York: Random House, 1969.

Norris, Frank. *McTeague.* New York: Doubleday, 1899.

Paley, Grace. *Enormous Changes at the Last Minute.* New York: Farrar, Straus & Giroux, 1974.

————. "Other People's Children." *Ms.* 4 (September 1975): 68–70, 95–96. Collected in *Just as I Thought.* New York: Farrar, Straus & Giroux, 1998, 111–21.

Rosen, Gerald. "Dreams of a Jewish Batboy." In Klinkowitz, *Writing Baseball,* 50–57.

Rosenberg, Harold. "The American Action Painters." In *The Tradition of the New.* New York: Horizon, 1959, 23–39.

Stephens, Michael. *Green Dreams: Essays under the Influence of the Irish.* Athens: University of Georgia Press, 1994.

————. *Lost in Seoul.* New York: Random House, 1990.

————. *Season at Coole.* New York: Dutton, 1972; reprinted in paperback editions since 1984 by the Dalkey Archive Press, Normal, IL.

————. "Why I Hate Baseball." In Klinkowitz, *Writing Baseball,* 70–77.

Sukenick, Ronald. "The Death of the Novel." In *The Death of the Novel and Other Stories.* New York: Dial, 1969, 41–102.

————. *In Form: Digressions on the Act of Fiction.* Carbondale: Southern Illinois University Press, 1985.

————. "Momentum." In *The Death of the Novel and Other Stories,* 9–40.

————. *Wallace Stevens: Musing the Obscure.* New York: New York University Press, 1967.

Vonnegut, Kurt. *Cat's Cradle.* New York: Holt, Rinehart & Winston, 1963.

————. *Mother Night.* Greenwich: Fawcett, 1962.

————. *Slaughterhouse-Five.* New York: Delacorte Press/Seymour Lawrence, 1969.

————. "Up Is Better Than Down." *Vogue* 156 (August 1970): 144–45. Collected as "Address to the Graduating Class at Bennington College, 1970," in *Wampeters, Foma and Granfalloons.* New York: Delacorte Press/Seymour Lawrence, 1974, 159–68.

————. *Welcome to the Monkey House.* New York: Delacorte Press/Seymour Lawrence, 1968.

Walker, Alice. *In Love and Trouble: Stories of Black Women.* New York: Harcourt Brace Jovanovich, 1973.

————. "Remembering Mr. Sweet." *New York Times Book Review* (May 8, 1988): 33. Collected as "The Old Artist: Notes on Mr. Sweet," in *Living by the Word.* New York: Harcourt Brace Jovanovich, 37–40.

Waugh, Evelyn. *The Loved One.* London: Chapman & Hall, 1948.

Wilson, Robley. "Favorites." In *Terrible Kisses.* New York: Simon & Schuster, 1989, 91–96.

Wolff, Rick. "Triumphant Return." In Klinkowitz, *Writing Baseball,* 103–8.

Jerome Klinkowitz, a professor of English and University Distinguished Scholar at the University of Northern Iowa, is the author of forty books, including novels, collections of short stories, and studies of literature, philosophy, art, music, sport, and air combat narratives.